W9-BBL-512

this journal belongs to

Britta Vorhies

date I started this study

August 29, 2005

COMMUNITY
THE NEW TESTAMENT CHURCH
THE ESSENCE OF FELLOWSHIP

COMMUNITY
THE NEW TESTAMENT CHURCH
THE ESSENCE OF FELLOWSHIP

By Adam Robinson

Student Life Publishing, Inc.
Birmingham, AL

Copyright © 2005 • Student Life Publishing, Inc.

No part of this publication may be reproduced in any form without the prior written permission of the publisher except in the case of brief quotations within critical articles and reviews.

ISBN 0-9755697-4-0

Unless otherwise noted, all Scripture quotations are taken from the Holy Bible, New International Version. Copyright © 1973, 1978, 1984 by International Bible Society. Used by permission. All rights reserved.

Printed in the United States of America.

Student Life Publishing, Inc.
P.O. Box 36040
Birmingham, AL 35236

To order additional copies of this resource, call the publisher at 888.811.2072 or order online at www.studentlifebiblestudy.com.

Inside images © BananaStock, Comstock, and Photodisc.

Table of **Contents**

Editorial and Design
Staff

Executive Editor
Paul Kelly

General Editors
Andy Blanks
Jill Puckett

Associate Editor
Lynn Waldrep

Art Director
Drew Binkley

Graphic Design
Liz Gibson,
Gibson Graphiks,
lizgibson@earthlink.net

Cover Design
Jason Lazzaro
Drew Binkley

Author

Adam Robinson—Being a Christian should be fun, but it's not easy. Along the way we all need people to help us take the next step in our journey with Christ. Helping students find that next step has been the backbone of Adam Robinson's ministry since day one. For the past eight years he's been traveling and preaching at camps, conferences, revivals, and other events. And while eight years of camp food isn't good for anyone, he still enjoys traveling and speaking full time. Adam began working with Student Life in 1997 when he started as a seminar speaker, camera operator, truck loader, and general grunt worker. Since then, Student Life has been gracious enough to not make him pack trucks anymore and instead allows him to serve as camp pastor.

Adam grew up in a solid Christian home in Montgomery, Alabama. Like may students who grow up in church, though, Adam found his walk with Christ drifting into boredom and complacency. After a camp experience of his own, God helped him leave that boredom behind and enter into a walk with Jesus that has changed his life.

Adam attended Samford University where he narrowly avoided a career as a lawyer. He then wandered aimlessly for a few years before attending Beeson Divinity School where he earned a Master of Divinity degree. When not living out of his car and preaching, you can find Adam in Birmingham, AL, catching up on his favorite hobbies, that include photography, storm chasing, disc golf, and swimming with Great White sharks. OK, maybe not the last one, but it is on his to-do list. You can contact Adam and learn more about his ministry at www.adamrobinson.org.

Doctrinal Statements

Do you know what a "doctrine" is? It is a truth or principle that is foundational to the faith of a person or group. As Christians we discover our core truths—our doctrines—in the Bible. A number of these core truths are presented in the Bible. At Student Life, we have identified eight biblical doctrines we believe are essential for every Christian to know and understand. These statements are descriptions of those essential biblical truths and have been developed to help you talk about your faith. They will help you know what you believe!

God is the one true living God, infinite, all-knowing, perfect in all His attributes, One in essence, eternally existing in three Persons—the Father, Son and Holy Spirit.

The Bible is God's Word, truth without any mixture of error, totally sufficient and completely authoritative for matters of life and faith.

People are God's Treasure, fashioned in His image, born with a sin nature and into an environment inclined toward sin. Only by the grace of God through Jesus Christ can they experience salvation.

Jesus is God and Savior, fully God and fully human. As the Son of God, we believe in His deity, virgin birth, sinless life, miracles, atoning death, resurrection and coming return.

The Holy Spirit is God, the Presence and Power living within every Christian from the moment of salvation and securing them until Christ's return.

Salvation is by Faith Alone, wholly by grace on the basis of the redeeming work of Christ and not on human merit. All the redeemed are secure in Christ forever.

The Church is God's Plan, one united spiritual body of which Christ is the head. The Church's purpose is to glorify God by taking the gospel to the world and building its members in Christlikeness.

God Holds the Future and this hope motivates believers in their daily lives. One day Jesus Christ will return personally and visibly in glory to the earth.

community: The New Testament Church—The Essence of Fellowship

How To Use This Book

The purpose of this 48-week journal is to help you learn the story of the New Testament Church. Though the events surrounding the formation of the Church happened nearly 2,000 years ago, they are relevant today. You can still apply the biblical truths of those stories to your life as a 21st century Christian living as a member of the global Church. Through this journal, you will learn about being a member of your church as well as the Church made up of all the Christians in the world. This journal includes a few different sections in each week to help you as you learn. Here's how to use them:

Introductions These are short sections introducing each week of devotionals. If you are studying the COMMUNITY series on Sunday mornings, Wednesday nights or in small groups, each week of devotions will coincide with what you are studying in class. Read the introductions to get a picture of what the week's devotions will center on.

Daily Devotions Now we're getting to the good stuff! The journal is designed to walk you through five days of devotions per week. Each devotion has a Scripture passage and a paragraph of text. Always start by reading the Scripture passage from your Bible then read the text. Look for ways in which the text unlocks truths of Scripture you may not have noticed before.

Daily Questions After each devotional paragraph, there are questions designed to get you thinking.

When you read these questions, take a moment to really think about what they are asking. Listen to the Holy Spirit as He teaches you through Scripture. Then record your thoughts in the journal space.

Journal Space You will notice this book is different from many books you have read before. It is designed to be filled with your thoughts. Use the space provided to record your reactions to each devotional passage. Or use it to write a prayer request or praise to God. Use it anyway you please. It's your journal! There are no rules, just guidelines. The important thing is to listen to the Lord and open your heart in response to His leading.

If you take the time to read the devotionals prayerfully and with the anticipation that God will reveal new things to you, you will be amazed at what will flow through your pen or pencil onto the pages.

Introduction

It was a pretty amazing time to be a disciple. Jesus had already been crucified and raised from the dead. And in the beginning of Acts, we find Jesus and the disciples hanging out together. He had already told them to wait in Jerusalem for the Holy Spirit to come upon them, but this confused the disciples. So logically, they asked Jesus about it. Jesus calmly explained to them that it wasn't their place to know His plan; they'd know when it happened. And no sooner had the words left His mouth when, all of a sudden, He was gone. Ascended. Whisked away in the clouds. Wow . . . imagine that!

After three years of healings, preaching, and traveling, Jesus had been murdered, risen from the grave and then ascended back into heaven. And after all of that, there they were . . . eleven guys on a hillside, staring into the sky with one question in their minds . . .

"Now what?"

This is how the Book of Acts begins. More importantly, this is also how the Church began. The same church you are now a part of got started 2,000 years ago by those eleven guys. When Jesus ascended back into heaven it wasn't the end of the story, it was a whole new beginning. These guys thought they had seen it all. In God's eyes they had barely begun.

Maybe that's your story, too. Maybe you think you've seen it all. You're saved. You believe in God; believe in His Son, Jesus; and you go to church like you're supposed to. But what do you do now? What comes after being saved? How are you supposed to grow in your faith? That's where the church comes in.

God isn't just interested in making sure you are saved. That's the beginning, but there is much more in store for you. You may not know it, but when you became a son or daughter of God, you didn't just get adopted by the Heavenly Father. You also got adopted by a whole family of brothers and sisters. That family is the Church. God has a plan for your life, but it's not just for you . . . it's for all of us.

This year we're going to look at one of the most important aspects of our spiritual lives. In fact, it's so important that your spiritual walk will never really work without it. What is it? Community. I know, sounds kind of dry, but once you get a taste of it you'll wonder how you lived without it. Community isn't just going to church or wearing a Christian tee shirt or showing up for church events. It's much, much more.

Imagine the relationship you have with your few best friends. You talk, you hang out, you like them. If they were in trouble you'd help them out—no questions asked. If you were in trouble you know they would be there in a minute. And you probably

community: The New Testament Church—The Essence of Fellowship

tell them more about yourself than you tell other people. Why? Because you're connected. In a way you can't really put into words. It's just different from everyone else.

Now imagine having that kind of relationship with 10 people. With 50. With 500. Of course you couldn't spend all that time with each person, but imagine knowing that all of those people would be there for you in a heartbeat. Imagine loving that many people and being willing to help them no matter what. Imagine not having to put up a mask for all those people because they all love you just the way you are. And every single one of them would be serving God and helping you to do the same. Now you're starting to see it: The Kingdom of God. His community.

The New Testament Church was just like that. What began as a disjointed, rag-tag group of unschooled men became the foundation for a force of change that would eventually touch all corners of the globe. The New Testament Church is your spiritual heritage. And although the events surrounding its formation took place almost 2,000 years ago, we can still learn so much today. It is an incredible story!

All this year we're going to look at how to build real community. We'll walk through the Book of Acts and see how it all began. We'll learn how to create that same kind of community right where we are.

It's a huge task but one that will shape everything about you and me and all of us—together.

So you may be asking yourself, "Now what?"

Well, turn the page and find out . . .

God's Army: What Is the Church?

memory verse

The stone the builders rejected has become the capstone; the LORD has done this, and it is marvelous in our eyes. **Psalm 118:22-23**

It started quietly enough. Off in a quiet corner Jesus asked a simple question of His trusted friends. Peter answered for all of them: "We believe you're the Son of God." They had little understanding of the meaning of that one simple statement. That confession was the foundation of a world-shattering new reality: God was present among them and was creating something that would change the world for all time. That reality is the Church of Jesus Christ.

Today you and I are the latest in an unbroken line of believers that started way back then. And what started on that day wasn't a movement, a cult, or a philosophy. Instead, God decided to build a family—a living, breathing family of millions—all linked through His Spirit. If you're saved, it's your family. God sent Jesus to be the head of a new nation of people, a nation without physical borders, racial divisions, or social barriers.

Welcome to the citizenship of the Spirit. Today all believers across the world form the Church, and small parts of that larger body meet together as local churches just like yours. This week we'll try to answer the question, "What is the church?" and find out how we fit in. We'll find that God has plans not just for you, but for all of us . . . together.

Day 1 >

Matthew 16:13-20

In His day, everyone was confused about who Jesus was and no one fully grasped His mission as the Messiah. Living on this side of history, grasping His mission may seem easier; we know the end of the story. But lots of people are still confused about Him today. Some think He's just a teacher, others think He's one of many pathways to heaven, still others think He's a lunatic. Some people don't think He existed at all. Before we can be a part of the Church we have to answer this question for ourselves: "Do I really believe He is the Son of God and that He can save me from my sins?" The only way into the Church is to confess Jesus as Lord. Have you done that?

If no one you knew believed in Jesus, would you? Why?

If everyone you knew decided He wasn't really the Son of God, would you? Why?

Day 2 >>

Mark 10:17-31

This is one of those classic moments in Scripture—the moment where someone decided to leave everything and follow Christ. But put yourself in Peter's shoes. He had already said yes, already left his home and job. He was able to do what the rich young ruler wasn't. Jesus told him that he would receive a hundredfold "in this present age" of what he had left behind. So how does that work? Peter wasn't the father of hundreds by the time he died. Jesus was trying to help us understand that when you join Him, you join His family. Through Christ we become connected to all other believers. So instead of just being on your own, all of us in the Church support and love one another. You already have lots of fathers, mothers, brothers, and sisters just because you are part of your church. Welcome to the family!

Have you made the kind of choice Peter did?

How are you building relationships with the people in your church?

Day 3 >>>
1 Corinthians 12:27-31; Colossians 1:18

Being a part of a family means different things as you grow up. At first you just have a name, and as you grow you take on more responsibility. But you never lose the name. Paul in these passages told us a lot about who we are as a Church. First, he let us know who the boss is. Jesus is the head of the church. Not a pastor or a group of men—only Jesus Himself. But

inside that church every one of us has a role to play, just like each part of your body has a specific function. Jesus functions as the authority of the church as well as the glue that holds it together, but you have a unique role to fill that no one else can. Without you, the Church won't work like Jesus wants it to. And that makes you indispensable.

How can you honor Jesus today as head of His Church?

Do you know what your role in the Church is? Ask Christ to show you.

Day 4 >>>>
1 Peter 2:9-10

Do you know your heritage? Perhaps there are Native Americans in your lineage—or Scottish blood. Knowing that you are part of a larger family gives you a sense of place in the history of the world, letting you know you are not just the new kid on the block. You may not know your human heritage, but you can know your spiritual heritage. Peter, a Jew, reminded all the believers in his church regardless of their race that because they belonged to Christ they were a part of God's people and members of His Kingdom. This is your spiritual heritage. Being a Christian is not just about knowing Jesus. It's about being a part of what God is doing in all of us all over the world. How does it feel to know you are a part of a larger spiritual Kingdom?

Since you are a part of this Kingdom, how should this change the way you live as a believer?

Day 5 >>>>>
Ephesians 5:25-32

You're probably not married, but follow me on this one. Paul is trying to show us what being the Church is like, and he uses marriage as the example. Jesus is the groom and the church is the bride. Notice that you alone are not the bride, but all Christians together. God is preparing all of us that we might be His spotless bride. Reread the passage and look at how Jesus cares for His Church. God cares tremendously about the health of your church. Your particular church may have problems, but God is in the process of making us pure, holy, and unified. How is Jesus doing this in the life of your church?

How should we as the Church respond to Christ if He is the groom?

If this is how God cares for His Church, how should we treat the other members of our local church?

The Power of the Spirit
Jesus' Ascension and the Holy Spirit

memory verse

"But you will receive power when the Holy Spirit comes on you; and you will be my witnesses in Jerusalem, and in all Judea and Samaria, and to the ends of the earth." **Acts 1:8**

Graduation Day! Can you imagine how great it is going to feel to be done with school, be more in charge of your own schedule, and enjoy your freedom? But then again, it's kind of comfortable where you are. You have a schedule, life is predictable, you know everyone, and you know where everything is. Do you really have to leave all that behind?

In Acts 1:4-14, the disciples were kind of like that. They had gotten used to having Jesus around. They were probably thrilled about this promised Holy Spirit, but secretly I'll bet they wished things could just stay the same. Couldn't Jesus hang around a little longer? But in order to achieve His plan for the spread of the gospel, Jesus had to leave His friends. He wanted them to experience the fullness of a relationship with Him and to have the power to spread the Word throughout the region and the world! For that they would need the Holy Spirit.

This week we're going to look at what Jesus had to say about the promised Holy Spirit and how He works in our lives. He is our intimate link to the Father, and everything we need is found in Him. The Holy Spirit that was promised to the disciples is the Holy Spirit that lives in each of us, so it's important we know how to live in Him. Get ready, because He may be more than you bargained for.

Day 1 >

Acts 1:4-14

I don't like to wait, and I'm sure the disciples didn't either. Can you imagine waiting for this promise to be fulfilled? I wonder what they expected. Whatever they thought was coming, one thing they knew for sure was it would be powerful.

When the Holy Spirit came on them they had power to accomplish whatever God asked of them. This is important for us to remember, too. God is not asking you to just give Him your best shot at ministering to others. He sends His Spirit to help us accomplish every task He assigns. Our job is to rely on Him for all our power needs and stop trying to accomplish life on our own. It's hard to give up your control, but the results will prove it's well worth it.

Do you truly believe that God will empower you through the Spirit to accomplish anything?

How are you relying on God's Spirit to live the Christian life today?

Day 2 >>

John 16:5-11

Jesus knew how the disciples would feel without Him around. So here He explained to them how the Spirit would work in their lives. Even though He wouldn't be around physically the Spirit would continue to do all the things that Jesus had done. And because the Spirit would be in all believers that ministry took on a much larger scale. Jesus would still be doing His Father's work, He would just be doing it through the Holy Spirit. He is now doing the Father's work through the Holy Spirit that's in you. So in effect, He didn't leave. Jesus placed His Spirit in us so we can all join Him in His work, not just the first century disciples.

Do you believe that God can use you to accomplish His will? Do you think He will?

Ask the Father to use you today to advance the Kingdom.

Day 3 >>>

John 16:12-15

The disciples had gotten used to the luxury of having Jesus around. When they had a question, they could simply ask Him. But what would happen after His ascension? Jesus told them that the Spirit would continue to speak to them and help them understand everything they needed to know. Far from being silent, the Holy Spirit would be their constant guide to point them to Truth. Now we can have the same privilege the disciples had, talking to God whenever we want! The Spirit isn't just for the full-time church staff; He dwells in every single believer. So if you have become a Christian, this privilege is for you. The question for us is, are we listening?

Have you ever listened for the voice of the Holy Spirit in your life? How did you know it was Him?

Ask the Father to make the voice of the Holy Spirit very clear in your life.

Day 4 >>>>
John 14:25-27

So how do you hear the voice of the Holy Spirit? What exactly does He sound like? It will take some time to recognize it, but the clearest way to know you're hearing from God is to listen for Him in Scripture. Here Jesus told us that the Holy Spirit would remind us of all the things that Jesus said. We find those things revealed in God's Word. So when you are in a situation and all of a sudden Scripture comes to mind, you're most likely hearing the Holy Spirit. In order for Him to remind us of Scripture, we have to know Scripture.

community: The New Testament Church—The Essence of Fellowship

Reading our Bibles every day puts us in a great place to make sure we'll hear from the Holy Spirit. Do you read your Bible every day?

Has God ever spoken to you by reminding you of Scripture?

Ask the Father to remind you of things He wants you to know today.

Day 5 >>>>>>
Acts 1:8

Have you ever been given a job that seemed too much for you? That's probably how the disciples felt after hearing Jesus say this. They'd just been given the job of telling the whole world about Jesus. (Hey, no pressure there, right?) But Jesus, through the Spirit, was going to help them go and tell others about Him. Do you realize that this verse is directed toward you as well? He has given you the Spirit and now He wants you to do what the disciples did. That means telling others about our faith. Have you ever done that? Are you scared? So were they. But they did it, and they found out that the Spirit really did help them.

Pray today that you will have the opportunity to talk to someone about Jesus. You might be surprised at what happens.

The Church Founders
The Choosing of Mathias

memory verse

It was he who gave some to be apostles, some to be prophets, some to be evangelists, and some to be pastors and teachers, to prepare God's people for works of service, so that the body of Christ may be built up. **Ephesians 4:11-12**

Peter is a big figure in the Church. He is in paintings; he has a big church named after him, and apparently he got this sweet gig at the pearly gates. But back in the Book of Acts none of this was on his radar. In fact, all the disciples were a little confused. Jesus had always made the decisions, but suddenly the disciples were alone: fishermen, tax collectors, ordinary Joes. They must have thought, "We're here, but what are we supposed to do?"

They began working anyway, starting with the decision to replace Judas. Jesus had selected twelve disciples; it seemed important to them to continue to have twelve. Enter Mathias and Joseph. The disciples prayed that God would show them the right person, and He did. Mathias was chosen to replace Judas.

From there it's all history. Everything was happening according to God's plan. Little did they know they were the beginning of the Church of Jesus Christ. The church you attend this week can be traced back to these original followers of Christ.

This week we're looking at the apostles, people Paul referred to as the foundation of the Church. As we study them, try to put yourself in their shoes. Think what it would have been like to see the Church get started. Imagine how people might have treated them. Try to picture the kind of faith they must have had. Every story has a beginning, and yours goes all the way back to the disciples.

Day 1 >
Acts 1:15-26

Scripture doesn't record anything about either of these men outside of today's passage. But even in these few verses we find out a lot. We know Matthias had been traveling with the Lord from the beginning. He was an eyewitness to Jesus' ministry, death, and resurrection.

Would you have stuck with Jesus even if you hadn't been one of the chosen few? Matthias wasn't in the inner circle that Jesus originally picked, but he followed anyway. That says a lot. Remember, this was before Pentecost; the Holy Spirit hadn't arrived yet. Matthias was signing on to almost certain death. These are the kind of people God built His Church upon.

If Jesus gave you a chance to serve today, would you do it?

Will you follow Jesus no matter where He calls you?

Day 2 >>
2 Peter 1:16-19

Recently I met the general and the photographer who fought in the Battle of Ia Drang depicted in the movie *We Were Soldiers*. At that point, the movie wasn't a movie to me anymore; it was real life.

Everything I heard was more dramatic because I knew these guys had been there personally. In this passage Peter is reminding his readers that he was there. Everything they believed could be trusted because he has been an eyewitness. What we believe isn't a philosophy concocted by religious leaders; it's the truth! Peter wanted the believers to know they could trust the Scripture. He believed because he had seen things with his own eyes.

What are some of your experiences with Christ that remind you He's real?

Do you ever doubt the Scripture or choose not to believe?

How does this passage help you deal with those doubts?

Day 3 >>>
Ephesians 2:19-22

You may not think about it or even realize it, but you are a part of a long heritage of faith. The church you are now a part of didn't start with your parents, or even their parents, or those folks with gray hair in your church. No, you and I are part of a spiritual lineage that goes back about 2,000 years to Peter, John, and all the other disciples. It's a rich history, one that finds its roots in Jesus Christ. There aren't any apostles alive today nor will there be in the future, but Paul says that their teaching is the foundation of our faith, a foundation that Jesus Himself crafted. Think about all the famous believers throughout history: the apostles, St. Augustine, Martin Luther, Billy Graham. Do you realize that you are part of the same family tree that they are?

How does it feel to be in the same spiritual lineage as important Christians throughout history?

How is Jesus changing your life as He changed theirs?

Day 4 >>>>
Revelation 1:9-11

John was the brother of James and one of the inner three disciples (along with Peter and James) with whom Jesus shared the most. According to tradition he is the only apostle not to die a martyr's death. The passage you read today was most likely written around 95 A.D. By this time John was about 90 years old, and had been serving Christ for over 60 years. He'd watched almost all of his friends die and at this point, He was exiled alone on an island for his faith. But look what He was doing: he was having His own worship service! His devotion was such that nothing—not death, not torture, not long periods of suffering—could shake his faith. Why? Because he knew Jesus personally.

How does your relationship with Jesus help you deal with hard times?

Ask the Lord for help standing firm when things seem too much to bear.

Day 5 >>>>>

1 Timothy 3:1-12

I know what you're thinking: "I'm not a deacon!" But look at this for a moment. Who is supposed to lead the Church today? God raises up people from within the Church to lead it, but only certain people. These chosen leaders are not just your pastor or your youth minister; Paul was talking about normal people who step up to lead the church. That may be you one day. But to have that honor there are qualifications. The original apostles are no longer around, but we should live like they did. That's what these qualifications are about.

How many of these qualifications do you have already?

How many do you need to develop?

Is God calling you to lead in your world right now?

Do you know the deacons in your church? Find out who they are and ask one about what it means to be a leader in the church.

Baptism of the Spirit
The Holy Spirit at Pentecost

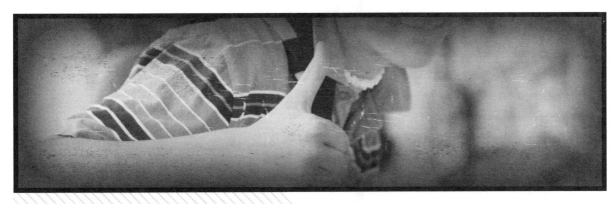

memory verse

Do you not know that your body is a temple of the Holy Spirit, who is in you, whom you have received from God? You are not your own; you were bought at a price. Therefore honor God with your body. **1 Corinthians 6:19-20**

It was dramatic. Rushing wind . . . pyrotechnics . . . crowds reeling in amazement . . . and one of the most effective sermons ever preached. This is how the Church was born at Pentecost. In one day over 3,000 people began the Church in Jerusalem.

Those believers were the start of something big. Since then the church has faithfully passed the message of Jesus Christ from generation to generation throughout the ages. Eventually someone told you. The church you are now a part of grew from the message of Christ the early Christians presented thousands of years ago.

The Holy Spirit of God made a surprise entrance at Pentecost, assuring us that from then on we would be able to do things that before would have been impossible. The Spirit now empowers us, guides us to the truth, teaches us, and helps us share our faith. With Him, amazing things are suddenly a possibility.

As believers, one of our main tasks is to remain connected to the Holy Spirit. This week we'll look at how the Spirit helps us and find out how to take advantage of the many miraculous opportunities He gives us every day.

Day 1 >

Acts 2:1-4; Ephesians 1:13-14

I don't know about you, but I've never seen tongues of fire. Ever. On anyone. So how do we know we have the Spirit in our lives? The disciples got this grand miracle. What about us? Paul tells us in Ephesians that we receive the Spirit when we first believe in Jesus Christ and become Christians. You have the Spirit right now. And even though you may not have seen a grand miracle like the apostles did when they received the Spirit, that same Spirit is in you. The Spirit empowered the early disciples and He will do that for us as well. The real question is, will we rely on Him?

Think back on some of the moments where you knew the Spirit was working in your life. How can we stay in touch with the Spirit on a continual basis?

Are you doing those things?

Day 2 >>

Ephesians 5:18

This is one of those verses that can be a little confusing. Don't we already have the Spirit? Then why do we need to be filled again? Did He leave? Absolutely not! Paul knows that every believer has the Holy Spirit dwelling in him, but He also knows

that he or she won't always rely on the Holy Spirit. While the Spirit is always with us, we choose every day whether we want Him to be in control. We can be filled with ourselves or we can be led by the Spirit. Paul reminded us to choose to be filled with God's Spirit each day rather than just doing our best on our own.

Would you describe your life as being filled with the Spirit? Why or why not?

Ask the Father today to help you empty yourself and be filled with the Spirit.

Day 3 >>>
Ephesians 3:14-21

This was Paul's prayer for the Ephesians, and I'd be willing to say it's God's desire for us. Read it through a few times. No really, read it again.

What are some of the things Paul wants to happen to us? In verse 16, Paul said the Spirit will strengthen your soul. Verse 17 tells us why: so we can have a deeper walk with Jesus. Verse 18 says we will have power when we dwell on the amazing love God has for us. In verse 19 Paul said if this happens we can be filled completely with God and His power. This is a pretty amazing prayer! All of this is for you. Why don't you pray this for your life?

Ask God to do the things for you that are mentioned in today's Scripture passage.

Pray this prayer for your friends, family, and church as well.

Day 4 >>>>

Ephesians 6:18-20

Why did Paul ask for prayer? Isn't he, you know, Paul? Super-Christian Paul? Paul knew that the Spirit wasn't just in him but in all his Christian friends as well. God is doing something in all of us—together. This means Paul couldn't be a loner; he needed the help of others. So when you face problems, it's important to ask for help—not just from God but also from God's people. Why? Because God's Spirit is in all of us. That's why Paul could ask them to pray "in the Spirit." So your prayers for others and theirs for you are incredibly powerful. Paul needed those prayers, and we need our friends' prayers as well.

Do you ever ask people to pray for you? Do you really think it will accomplish anything?

Do you ever pray for others?

Do you really think it helps?

community: The New Testament Church—The Essence of Fellowship

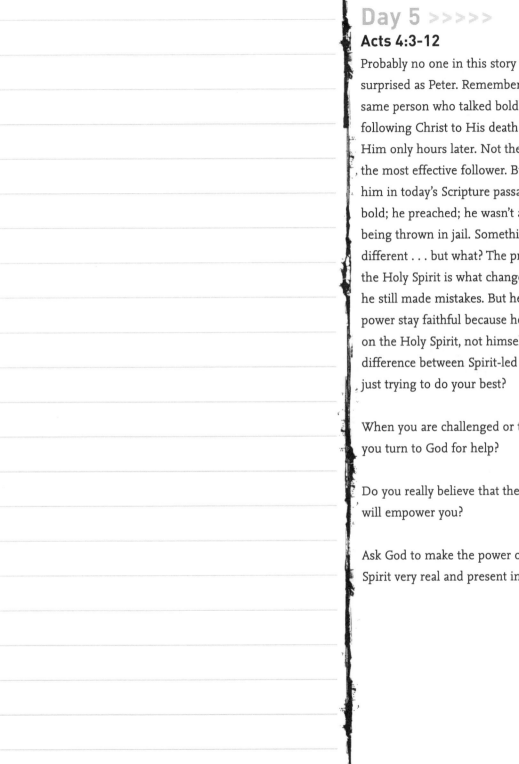

Day 5 >>>>>

Acts 4:3-12

Probably no one in this story was as surprised as Peter. Remember, this is the same person who talked boldly about following Christ to His death then denied Him only hours later. Not the picture of the most effective follower. But look at him in today's Scripture passage. He was bold; he preached; he wasn't afraid of being thrown in jail. Something was different . . . but what? The presence of the Holy Spirit is what changed Peter! Yes, he still made mistakes. But he had the power stay faithful because he was relying on the Holy Spirit, not himself. See the difference between Spirit-led living and just trying to do your best?

When you are challenged or tempted, do you turn to God for help?

Do you really believe that the Holy Spirit will empower you?

Ask God to make the power of the Holy Spirit very real and present in your life.

The Church's Message
Peter Speaks

memory verse

"God has raised this Jesus to life, and we are all witnesses of the fact." **Acts 2:32**

"**M**an Raised From the Dead!" It sounds like something you'd read in the *National Enquirer* or some crazy New Age book. But this fact is the basis for Christianity. The heart of the gospel is not a list of rules or regulations. It's Jesus' message that we need—and can have—a new life. And this new life is available to anyone who believes Jesus died and arose from the dead.

In Acts 2:14-33, Peter followed up the incredible baptism of the Holy Spirit with an awesome Pentecost sermon. He spoke the truth about the Holy Spirit . . . that God had promised it and kept His promise. And then he boldly proclaimed that the Jesus they had all watched die was alive again. More than anything else, this defined the beliefs of the apostles and the early Church. Without the resurrection there is no Christianity because Christ would still be dead.

The truths about Jesus contained in Peter's sermon have always been the Church's central message; it should be a message we claim for ourselves. Because Jesus is alive we can have a personal relationship with Him and know that He is working in our lives on a daily basis. It gives us confidence in the hope that one day we, too, will be resurrected. This week we'll look at what the resurrection means to us on a daily basis.

Day 1 >
Luke 24:36-48

Time for a reality check. Do you actually believe that Jesus rose from the dead? Think about this truth—not a story and not a sermon illustration, but that Jesus actually died and three days later walked out of a tomb. This is the message of the Church—that Jesus is alive today because He actually rose from the grave. But it makes no difference in your life unless you believe it yourself. If you have questions, ask a parent or a youth leader. But figure it out, no matter what it costs you. Note that the disciples themselves took a little convincing. Jesus wants you to have a faith of your own.

Ask the Lord to show you the truth and help you believe and understand it.

Day 2 >>
Colossians 1:9-12

Have you ever felt as if your prayers were bouncing off the ceiling . . . as if no one were really listening? Some people think we're stupid for praying to an invisible God. But the resurrection changes things. We don't pray to a dead god. Our God rose from the dead and is alive today, which means you can have a real relationship with Him. Knowing and obeying Him is not just about rules; it's about getting to know Him personally. The word *knowledge* in these verses means having an experience with someone, not just knowing facts. Jesus is alive and seeking a real relationship with you. Are you doing the same with Him?

Check your prayers. Do you pray as if someone is listening and might talk back?

Are you building a real relationship with Jesus?

Day 3 >>>

2 Corinthians 5:17

This is one of those verses to memorize. Make sure you underline it in your Bible. Think about it for a minute: when Jesus rose from the dead, He had a brand new life. He wasn't a mutilated man anymore; He received a new body and a new life.

When you became a Christian, that's what happened to you. You may look the same on the outside, but something cataclysmic has happened in your soul. You are a new creation. You will see Jesus face to face one day. And you have the power of God inside you. You didn't join a club or just decide to live differently. When you became a Christian, you became a true child of God. Wow! What a change!

Dwell on this verse throughout the day and think about what it really means.

Day 4 >>>>
Ephesians 1:17-21

Sometimes I feel as if it is impossible to live the kind of Christian life I should. Following God is just really hard sometimes. But look at what Paul said here. He said the same power that God used to raise Jesus from the dead is working in us right now. The same power! The resurrection is the greatest miracle of all time, and that's the kind of power God is using in our lives! Our power doesn't always work, but His power always succeeds. No matter who you are, if you are in Christ, that same power is working in you.

Are there any places in your life where you are relying on your own strength instead of God's?

Choose today to actively rely on God's power instead.

Day 5 >>>>>
Acts 4:32-35

This is an interesting Scripture passage. Lots of good things are going on among the Christians: miracles, love, sharing. But look at verse 33. Many times I hear believers hurling insults at lost people for their behavior. But that wasn't the message of the early Christians. They always started with a new life in Jesus. He was alive, and they preached the message of new life in Him. The same is true for us: Before we can talk about behavior, we have to talk about new life! Without that power no one will see Jesus in us.

When we talk about Jesus, do we rely on His power?

When you share your faith, do you talk more about rules and guidelines of what Christians should or shouldn't do—or a relationship with God?

Is your life more about rules or a relationship with God through Jesus?

The Church in the World
Creating the Church

memory verse

And let us consider how we may spur one another on toward love and good deeds. Let us not give up meeting together, as some are in the habit of doing, but let us encourage one another—and all the more as you see the Day approaching. **Hebrews 10:24-25**

What do you think of when you hear the word *church*? Steeples? Sundays? Sermons? All of these are fine, but they aren't church. In fact, they never have been. They help the church, but they aren't actually the church.

After Peter's sermon in Acts 2, thousands of people responded by repenting and being baptized. These first believers had no buildings or steeples and initially didn't even meet on Sunday. They began eating together, meeting together, loving one another, and worshiping wherever they could. Church wasn't a place; Church was what they were when they gathered together as God's people.

So what is the Church? The Church is you! Actually, it's you and all the other believers you know. Literally, believers are the Church.

You don't always need your minister around to do church. You can have church in your school, at home, or while hanging out with your friends. Being a part of the Church means living as a part of the believing community. So when you and your friends get together at school and help each other follow Christ better, you're being the Church together.

This week we are going to look at living as a church no matter where we are.

Day 1 >

Acts 2:37-47; 4:32-36

Can you believe this? Think about what
it would look like. There are over 3,000
Christians already, and no one kept their
stuff private. Why? They figured out that it
wasn't about them as individuals anymore.
It was about all of them together. Here's
a thought: Your relationship with God is
personal but not private. God is doing
something in us—all of us together—so
when we help our fellow believers, we're
really helping ourselves as well. We live
in a pretty selfish culture, so this kind of
thinking takes a while to sink in. We have
to start somewhere. Would you be willing
to give up some of your stuff to help your
friends and family at church? What about
the people you don't know quite as well?

What are some ways you can be less
selfish today?

What are some ways you could provide
for someone today?

Ask God to give you opportunities today.

Day 2 >>

John 4:19-24

Most of us know what to do depending on
where we are. In school we learn, on the
field we play, and in church we worship.

community: The New Testament Church—The Essence of Fellowship

Most of the time these things don't overlap. However, it's different with worship. We can miss out if we confine our worship to a time or place. In talking to the woman at the well, Jesus began referring to a new time—our time—when worship wouldn't be confined to one place or another. And He is looking for people who will worship Him no matter where they are. Since we are the Church, we should honor God no matter where we are: school, home, a ball game . . . anywhere.

The early Christians gathered in many places publicly to worship, pray, and encourage one another. Do you?

How can you worship God today in your daily routine?

Where are some places you could gather with other believers to talk about Him?

Day 3 >>>
2 Timothy 2:22

Have you ever read a passage and said to yourself, "I can't do that"? Let's be honest: Some things are easy during your quiet time but get a lot harder when you walk out your door. But look at Paul's advice here. I'm sure you're not shocked by the call to run away from evil youthful desires. But read the rest of the verse. God doesn't expect us to tackle this life alone. Our

Father provides godly people around us to help us along. You need Christian friends to help you through, and they need you.

Do you have this kind of friends?

Are you looking for them?

Think about the things this passage asks us to do. Pray today about how you and your believing friends could do them together.

Day 4 >>>>
Colossians 3:15-17

Verse 17 in today's passage is one of those verses I always thought I understood. It sounds pretty straightforward, doesn't it? Just do everything for God. But in the original language (Greek) the word "you" is plural. In fact, every time you see the word "you" in this passage, it's not talking about you alone. It's referring to the whole Church. Now that changes things entirely. I'm not just expected to walk with God by myself; I'm supposed to do it with other people. I need them, and they need me. That's why verses 15-16 read as they do.

Are you talking to others about what you read in the Bible?

Do you have the kind of friendships where that kind of thing just happens?

Who are some people you can work together with to follow Christ? Pray that God will strengthen your friendships today.

Day 5 >>>>>
1 Corinthians 5:9-11

Paul gave us some useful guidance. There have been a lot of believers who didn't want to have anything to do with lost people. Many Christians only hang out with other Christians and have forgotten how to get along with the rest of the world. Jesus never intended for us to do that, as Paul stated here. But he had strong words for those who claim to be Christians but act like the world. He said that if they don't act like believers, they shouldn't be treated like believers. God is building a real family among us, but we cannot condone people who say one thing and do another. The goal is not to condemn hypocrites but to help them see that they can't have it both ways. You have to choose which family you want to belong to and then act accordingly.

Is there someone you need to confront in love about his or her behavior?

Pray that God will give you wisdom and love to challenge your friend.

Physical Opposition
Peter, John, and the Sanhedrin

memory verse

But we are not of those who shrink back and are destroyed, but of those who believe and are saved. **Hebrews 10:39**

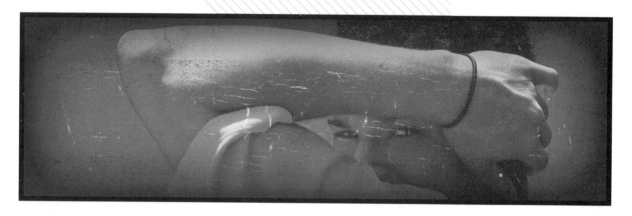

At the entrance to the Coliseum in Rome stands a huge iron cross. It was erected to commemorate the countless number of Christians who were killed for sport in that place and throughout the Roman Empire. Scary as it may seem, people have given their lives throughout history just for claiming to be Christians and refusing to deny Jesus. And while the Coliseum may seem millions of miles from your daily life, persecution and death are a present-day reality for many Christians around the world right now.

Peter and John knew this kind of persecution. In Acts 4:1-12, they were thrown in jail just because they were preaching the gospel. And that was just the beginning.

Your life may never be at risk simply because you are a Christian. But one of the things we will have to deal with as Christians is opposition. Jesus said that since people hated Him they would hate us as well for no other reason than we love God. It seems odd, but it happens.

You've probably already experienced people who will exclude you or make fun of you just for your beliefs. This week we're going to look at some responses to physical threats and how we can best use these situations to be witnesses for Christ.

Day 1 >
Acts 4:1-12

No one said this was going to be easy. Peter and John got a taste of what was to come. The majority of religious leaders all got together to point these guys out and tell them to shut up—or else. It had to be intimidating to stare down men who were more educated and tell them they were missing the point. Peter and John wouldn't back down, even though they were threatened. People will pressure you—verbally, silently, or even physically—to be quiet about Christ. At times like that you can't rely on your own power; you have to rely on God's power to give you courage and strength to stand firm. See how Peter relies on the Spirit in verse 8?

How do you respond when people try to intimidate you? Do you rely on Christ for your response?

Ask God to give you courage to stand firm when things get tough.

Day 2 >>
Acts 5:17-42

They did what? How could you be excited about being flogged? Flogging, by the way, was not like a spanking from your dad. It was extremely brutal and painful. So why were they excited? Jesus had warned them that this would happen—that they would follow in His footsteps and be physically persecuted. When they were beaten as Jesus was, and for the same reasons, they knew they were on the right track. They had a joy that was more important than the pain they were feeling. They didn't go out looking for a beating, but they endured it because Jesus had done the same thing. It's never fun to deal with persecution, but we at least can rejoice that we are walking in the footsteps of Jesus when it happens.

Why is it hard to praise in the midst of suffering?

What can you focus on when you find yourself in a similar situation?

Day 3 >>>
Acts 16:22-30

Here's another story of people being happy after a beating. Look today, though, at how Paul responded. After Paul prayed, God sent a miraculous earthquake to set them free. But when the doors opened, Paul and Silas stayed put. What was the deal? Well, look at the result. Paul could have thought about himself and walked out head held high, saying, "See what my God can do?" But instead he thought about the jailer (who got saved—along with his whole family). Jesus never lets an opportunity escape to show His love for people. When you get physically intimidated or hurt for the name of Christ, it's very natural to think about just yourself. Paul knew that God could use his beating to see someone saved. This in no way means that God wants those things to happen to you, but we have to look at the bigger picture when things like this occur.

Why did Paul have such little regard for himself?

Ask the Lord to show you how He can bring good out of some seemingly bad situations in your life right now.

Day 4 >>>>
Revelation 5:9-11

Stephen is recorded as the first martyr of the Christian church. The word *martyr* literally means *witness*. Those who are killed for being believers in Jesus are being witnesses to a lost world that Christ is real. You may not hear a lot about martyrs today, but believers all over the world literally risk their lives daily in parts of the world by proclaiming to be Christians. Believe it or not, there were more Christians martyred in the twentieth century than in all other centuries combined! And it's happening right now. At this very moment people are being persecuted just like the disciples were in the Book of Acts. Take some time today to remember those who are giving their lives for the sake of Jesus. Pray for their protection, pray for their families, and pray that God would use their witness to bring others to faith in Christ.

Go to www.persecution.com for more information about what is happening in the world with Christians in other countries right now.

Day 5 >>>>>
Hebrews 10:32-39

Let's be honest: when things get dangerous, or even uncomfortable, we can get scared. That's OK. Anyone in an intimidating situation will feel that way. The author of Hebrews knew that, so he encouraged his readers to stand firm. Jesus isn't asking you never to fear; He's asking you to stand firm even when you are afraid. This is called perseverance. It means not giving in when you really want to. All of us will face moments we think we can't handle. If you stand firm convinced Christ is with you, you'll be surprised what you can endure. This is the essence of faith: refusing to give in because you know God is watching over you.

Look in this passage and find the reasons why you can stand firm.

Ask the Lord to show you how to have faith in hard situations.

One Community
Sharing Among Believers

memory verse

Be devoted to one another in brotherly love. Honor one another above yourselves.
Romans 12:10

Growing up in church, the word *fellowship* meant some sort of gathering after the worship service that involved food. That was about it. It seemed pointless then, but looking back I can see how important those times were. A church is a family made up of different types of people. The only way that kind of group can become a real family and not just a crowd is to spend time together.

This week we'll see them giving money to one another, sharing their possessions, and taking care of one another. This is what a real church family is supposed to look like. But how do we get there?

In every church God wants to build something called *community*, the sense that we are all connected in a real way. Serving each other, helping, loving, and giving are all ways we express real community.

Believe it or not, this can be the most exciting and life-changing aspect of your church experience. But community isn't easy to come by. It takes a deliberate choice to be a part of the people of God. Once you join, the benefits are endless. This week we're going to look at how to build real community in our own churches.

Day 1 >

Acts 4:32-37

Sharing isn't natural. No one has to teach a child to be selfish with his toys. That trait just comes naturally to him. But it applies to teenagers and adults as well. So how do you figure 3,000 people voluntarily selling their possessions to help other people? When the Spirit of God moves, we find out He provides all we need. He even provides us with a family of parents, brothers, and sisters to help us through life. Recognizing God's provision, Barnabas gladly chose to sell his land to aid the church. Would you be willing to do the same with your stuff? Our culture is selfish; it's time we challenged it by loving each other sacrificially.

Do you believe God will provide all you need—even when you give to help others?

Do you truly love the people in your church?

What are some ways you can serve the people in your church this week?

Day 2 >>

Ephesians 3:25-32

If you have a brother or sister, you know that living with other people can be tough. It can be even harder for large families to get along. So imagine the problems that can

community: The New Testament Church—The Essence of Fellowship

arise in a church of hundreds or thousands of people. Paul encouraged the church at Ephesus to be unified, but as in any family problems sometimes arose.

Go back and read this passage carefully. Think about each command Paul gave. Ask God to help you identify any situation where you might need to change your actions. Remember, these aren't just rules; God is trying to help us have healthy relationships with Him and one another.

Day 3 >>>
James 5:13-16

Almost everyone has secrets—sins, issues, problems we don't want to talk about. When we pretend we don't, we are not actually being truthful with our friends. One of the ways we build community is by being honest with one another. In today's Scripture passage, James commanded us to confess our sins not only to God but to one another. Why? Because God uses each of us to help our friends in Christ. He's not saying we should tell everyone, but rather we should be accountable to other trusted Christian friends. The result is a depth of friendship you may have never experienced. I know it sounds terrifying, but we have to trust that God knows what He's doing. Believe me, I've tried it and it actually works. Confession of sins to each other is amazingly powerful.

What are some things you struggle with that you've never told anyone about?

Who are some mature Christians you trust that you could talk to about these things?

Pray that God would show you who these people are and give you the courage to be honest with them.

Day 4 >>>>
1 Thessalonians 1:1

What can you possibly get out of an introduction? A lot, actually! Flip through your New Testament and look at the first verses of some of the letters Paul wrote. Notice anything? Paul rarely wrote a letter alone. It's always Paul and Timothy, Paul and the brothers, or Paul and Sosthenes. Why did Paul always mention these people if he was doing all the writing? Well, Paul wasn't a loner. He knew he needed other people—his community—to fully follow God. And so do we. Walking with God isn't an isolated action.

If you had to write a letter to a group of Christians who lived far away, who would you put at the top of your letter? Who's walking beside you right now in your Christian journey? If no one comes to mind, maybe it's time to start cultivating more Christian friendships.

Thank God for the strong Christian friends that you have.

Ask God to show you ways you can grow closer to other Christians.

Day 5 >>>>>
Hebrews 10:24-25

I don't think any truly rational people like to get up early. I don't. Ever! But sometimes it's necessary. And there are occasions when I don't mind, like Christmas morning. For some reason, getting up early on Christmas has never bothered me. Sometimes it may seem like a chore to get up and make it to church on Sunday. What's the big deal? Why do we have to do that anyway? The big deal is that it's a chance for your community to meet together, and that doesn't happen often. They need to see you to encourage you, and they need you to do the same for them. The author of Hebrews knew that and reminded us how important this is. If we never met together we'd never grow into the kind of family God wants us to be. So get up! It's time to see the church. It's time to be the church!

Think about all the ways you are encouraged when you go to church.

Think about the people you can encourage. Ask God to help you remember these things each Sunday.

Integrity
Ananias and Saphira

memory verse

But just as he who called you is holy, so be holy in all you do.

1 Peter 1:15

Mahatma Gandhi was an influential Hindu leader in the early twentieth century whose life and teachings are still followed by many today. He often referred to Jesus in terms of praise, prompting someone to ask whether he would become a Christian. In reply, he said, "I like your Christ; I do not like your Christians. Your Christians are so unlike your Christ." His sentiment is shared by many. How many others have been driven away from church because some Christians talk like believers but never live out the faith they preach?

The reality is that if we don't live what we say, we lose our credibility in telling others about Jesus. When Christians lack integrity everyone loses. What's integrity? Having integrity means being honest. It means saying what you mean and meaning what you say. And it's more important than you know. In the early stages of the Church, God went so far as to kill one couple who purposefully lied to their church. What happened to them as a result was pretty drastic. But their lack of integrity threatened the Church.

As Christians we have to be diligent to make sure our lives reflect our beliefs. And since we're a part of a larger body, we have to help each other live out our beliefs as well. Even if we live correctly, if other believers are hypocrites it hurts our witnesses. So this week we're going to talk about the integrity of not just our lives but of the Church. Whether you like it or not, we're all in this together.

Day 1 >
Acts 5:1-11

Most of us have done things very similar to what Annanias and Sapphira did: commit some sin we don't think is important and then lie about it. So after reading this story, you should be fearful. God has every right to treat us the same way, so I thank Him for His mercy that He chooses not to. At times we may think we are getting away with some sin, but this story should remind us we are not. God may not choose to use His ultimate punishment, but He will not leave our sin unchecked. Hopefully this example will remind us that our sins are more damaging than we think and prompt us to avoid those sins.

Are there any sins in your life that you consciously accept? Why?

Ask God to show you where you are failing and thank Him for His grace to forgive you.

Day 2 >>
1 Corinthians 5:1-12

Today we get an answer to an important question: Should I ever judge someone? Most of us believe we should never judge people. In general this is a good rule; it keeps us from pridefully passing judgment on others. But the Corinthians adopted that rule and then let a hypocrite run wild among them. "Oh well, it's not my place to judge him," they might have said. Paul told them the opposite. We are not to judge unbelievers; they're lost. But when someone claims to be a believer in Christ and then deliberately acts in a way that dishonors Him, it is our duty to confront that person in love. Paul suggested a stern punishment that ultimately brought this person back to a pure walk with God.

Do you have friends who say they are Christians but don't act like it? How can you confront them in love?

Ask God to give you courage to not allow sin to go unchecked in your life, in the lives of your friends, or in your church.

Day 3 >>>
Revelation 3:14-18

I used to think this passage meant I should be hot and never cold for God. But read it again. The problem in Laodicea is not that they were wicked people; it's that they weren't really . . . anything. They talked a good game, but they were wishy-washy when it came to following God. God basically said to the church at Laodicea, "If you believe something, then act on it!" He says the same to us. If we claim to be Christians, we can't afford to be half-hearted,

saying one thing but never living it. It's not enough to simply avoid big sins and live with little ones. It dishonors God and sends a message to everyone we know that our Father really isn't all that important to us. How's your temperature?

Would you say that you are hot, cold, or lukewarm? Why?

Ask God to help you get off the fence and move toward a more focused walk with Him today.

Day 4 >>>>
Ephesians 5:1-8

Paul used an interesting phrase in this passage. He told us there shouldn't even be a *hint* of sexual immorality among God's people. Many Christians ask, "Well, how far can I go? How far is too far?" Paul told us we are asking the wrong questions; we are trying to get as close as we can to sin instead of safeguarding our integrity. God isn't opposed to sex; He honors sexual expression within the bounds of marriage. Until we marry, we are not to risk losing our integrity by pushing the envelope of what is too far. If we ignore Paul's advice, we'll find ourselves like Annanias and Sapphira regretting sins we knew we should have stayed away from (and paying the consequences that go with them).

What decisions have you made to remain sexually pure?

Who are the people who help you stay true to those commitments?

Day 5 >>>>>
Titus 2:3-8

Is what you do really important? Paul gave some good advice to Titus, a young pastor: to keep pure. But for ordinary people like us it's not as important, right? Actually it is. Twice in this passage, Paul told us to live holy lives and then gave us a reason: when people try to say bad things about us, they'll have no grounds for it. They'll look like the evil ones because there's nothing bad to say about us.

Our integrity is important because it paves the way for the gospel. If we're hypocrites, no one will listen to us when we try to tell them about Jesus. When our lives reflect what we believe, it opens the door for people to hear what we say about Christ.

Do you know people who won't believe in Christ because of Christians they know?

What can you do this week to change that image?

Ask God to give you an opportunity to do that this week.

community: The New Testament Church—The Essence of Fellowship

An Invincible Church
Persecution of the Apostles

memory verse

Peter and the other apostles replied: "We must obey God rather than men!" **Acts 5:29**

Let's think for a moment about all the religions that have come and gone. There were all those Egyptian gods, that whole druid thing, and how can we forget all those Greek gods? Poor guys, no one really worships them anymore. Oh well, rest in peace.

But then there's the Church. By Church (capital C), I mean all the believers in Jesus Christ around the world. Not only has the Church stood the test of time—

spanning over 2,000 years of history—but multitudes of people have tried to destroy it without success. Bibles have been burned, apostles executed—an entire empire tried to wipe the Church out—all to no avail. The Church continues to thrive. Why? Because Jesus is the Lord of lords and the King of kings. Imposters fade away while He remains.

The situation has been the same from the Church's beginning. In Acts, the apostles were threatened

by religious and government authorities; they were thrown in jail and beaten. But none of this put even a dent in God's unfolding plan for His Kingdom in the world. The Church continued to grow through all of the opposition.

Today's Church is the same way. Christians around the world are persecuted, and the Church of Jesus Christ still stands. Yet most of us don't see the Church as the invincible body it is.

Day 1 >

Acts 5:17-32

The apostles were jailed, freed by an angel, captured again, and brought before the people who imprisoned them. But through all this, they didn't even begin to water down their message. In fact, they did just the opposite. When asked why they had violated orders, they basically said the only One they obeyed was God. What if we had the same attitude? What if we weren't afraid of offending people or didn't care about our images? What if we were bold like the apostles and shared our faith without worrying about the consequences? Does this sound extreme? Truth is, this is exactly what we as the Church are supposed to be doing. God has given us the power. What are we doing with it?

You will face persecution as a Christian in today's society. What can you learn from today's story of the apostles?

God made you spiritually invincible. Pray that God will give you a spirit of boldness.

Day 2 >>

Acts 9:31; 12:24; 13:52; 16:5

You may not know the whole story of Acts, but flip through the headings and see what's going on. You'll see stonings, persecutions, and danger. Yet look at today's verses. These are like chapter markers in the Book of Acts showing how the gospel continued to move. No matter what happened, the Church continued to grow and thrive. Why? Because God was with them. God never said this was going to be easy, but He did say He would be with us. As the hardships increased for the early Church, the power of God sustained them and even helped them grow stronger. The same can be true for us today. When we seek to serve the Lord together and refuse to let circumstances stop us, we can count on the power of God making our lives and churches just as powerful.

What are some obstacles that have hindered your church or youth group?

Are these an insurmountable problems?

Ask God to empower your church as He did the churches in Acts.

Day 3 >>>
Romans 1:16-17

Why is the Church so powerful? It's not because of the people. There are some individuals who can command a crowd or get things done politically. But the power of the Church doesn't come from strong personalities; it comes from the gospel itself. You may feel weak or inadequate when trying to share the gospel, but you don't have to. The gospel is powerful all by itself. When witnessing to others concentrate more on the gospel and less on your shortcomings. They are not as limiting as you think they are. When our lives and our churches are committed to Christ, we don't need to be ashamed of anything.

Have you ever been ashamed of the gospel? Why?

How does this passage help you have confidence in sharing your faith?

Day 4 >>>>
Matthew 16:13-18

In today's passage, we find out that neither death, hell (*hades* is another word for hell), or the grave can stand up to the power of the gospel. But notice it's not just the gospel but also the Church that will never be defeated. Once we join Christ, we join His body—the Church. As a part of Christ Himself, we don't have to fear the power of death or hell. It literally can't overpower us. The church—your church—is much more powerful than you realize. We sell ourselves short when we assume that we can't do anything in the world. When we realize how strong we are, hell itself will tremble as we accomplish God's will!

How does this passage change the way

you look at your own church? Are there any places in your life where you just assumed you were defeated?

Ask God to show you how strong you are as a part of His Church.

Day 5 >>>>>
2 Corinthians 11:22-33

Can this be right? I don't know about you, but after the first two shipwrecks I'd be a little hesitant about getting on any more boats! But Paul was unstoppable. It didn't matter what he went through; he refused to back down. What makes a man do that? What makes someone willingly walk into a dangerous situation? In verses 28-29 Paul showed us why. He was so passionate about the Church that it was more important to him than his own comfort. God had changed his life and saved him from hell, and he wanted everyone to know that joy. God may never ask you to do things like this, but what would you be willing to endure just to tell someone about the gospel? The Church is invincible, but it can be weakened in the short term if we refuse to attempt the task God has set out for us.

What are some of the sacrifices you have to make to share the gospel?

Ask the Father to give you a passion that can't be quenched by bad circumstances.

Shared Ministry
Choosing the Seven

memory verse

Let us not become weary in doing good, for at the proper time we will reap a harvest if we do not give up.

Galatians 6:9

Moses was tired. He was listening to one disagreement after another. I imagine him mediating a dispute between two people who both claimed to have created manna soup first, and both wanted the patent on the recipe. People had been coming to Moses with these kinds of questions all day. And the line was still wrapped twice around the tent. Not even Santa had to deal with lines like this. "This is ridiculous," he thought. "I just can't keep this up." But he was the leader of Israel; wasn't settling disputes his job? If so, how does the leader of a million people in a desert go on vacation? Next in line was Moses' father-in-law with some advice of his own. "Moses, share the load. It's not all up to you." So he did, and he got that vacation.

Just like Moses, the apostles figured out early they coundn't do ministry by themselves. God helped them choose others to share the ministry of His Kingdom. Everyone in the early Church had a part to play in ministry.

This week we're going to think about the shared ministry of the Church. Whether you know it or not, God has a place for you to serve, and the whole concept of church won't work unless you get involved. It's time we all got off the pews and into the game!

Day 1 >

Acts 6:1-7

Michael Jordan is arguably the greatest basketball player of all time. But not even Jordan could have won a single game without his teammates. It's a lesson the Church should take to heart. God called out the apostles to a specific task, but many other tasks needed to be done. Unless others stepped up to the plate, the work wouldn't get done. God isn't about superstars hogging the entire ministry. In fact, when we let only a few people do the work, much less gets done. So if we are to truly accomplish God's will, we each have to find our place to serve—and then work at it with all of our hearts.

Do you see yourself having a vital role in your Church? If so, what is it?

How can you fulfill your specific task for the Kingdom today?

Day 2 >>

1 Corinthians 12:12-26

I really have no idea what my spleen does. I've never seen it, and to be honest, I hope I never do. But I thank God that I have one. My body—and life itself—would not be the same without it. I like my spleen! If the Church is a body, that means there is a place for hundreds of types of gifts. And if this body is going to function correctly, we need all of the people with those different gifts to be in place and working properly. You may not feel that your particular function in the church is all that important, but without your participation, everyone will suffer. God doesn't reserve ministry just for the church staff; all of us have a part to play! You may have a role that not a lot of other people see—like the spleen. But the fact that our vital organs are not visible doesn't make them unimportant!

Do you tend to downplay your importance in the church? Why?

How can you use your gift this week in a way that fits in with others using their gifts?

Day 3 >>>
1 Timothy 4:11-16

The letters Paul wrote to Timothy are different from the others he wrote. Letters like the one to the Ephesians, for example, were addressed to the whole church. But Paul's letters to Timothy were written just to him. So if it's advice just to Timothy, why are we reading it? I always wondered if I had to do these things Timothy was told to do since I wasn't a pastor like him. But Paul knew many more people should read this letter, so he wrote it accordingly. Even more, God must have wanted it read today since it appears in our Bible. That being said, when Paul told Timothy not to neglect his gift, everyone in the church would be reminded not to neglect his or her God-given gifts and ministries either. Re-read the passage and ask God to show you how this applies to you today.

Are you neglecting your gift(s)? How?

What can you do to use them in the church instead?

Ask the Father to help you do that today.

Day 4 >>>>
Galatians 6:2

We should try to memorize this verse. And while that shouldn't take too long, actually practicing it may take a lot longer! When we sit in a pew on Sunday, it's easy to get the idea that it's up to the pastor and paid staff to do all the real work of ministry. We're just here to help when we can, right? Not according to Paul! Echoing Jesus Himself, Paul reminded us that everyone should be involved in helping others. That means teaching one another, encouraging one another, serving one another, and praying for one another. You probably like one of these ministries more than the others. If so, you should make sure you work at that ministry to help others. This is the law of Christ: to love each other as we love ourselves. The church staff will never be able to do this without our help. How are you carrying others' burdens right now?

Ask God to show you how He can use you in others lives today, then keep your eyes open for opportunities.

Day 5 >>>>>
Acts 6:1-10

On Day 1 this week, we saw how the apostles selected seven men to clean tables and take care of the elderly in the church. You may have thought to yourself, "I'm glad I don't have that job." (I had the same reaction.) But one of these men—Stephen—was not only taking care of the widows, he was doing miracles! Since God was with him, Stephen saw the power of the Holy Spirit in everything he did. But even so, he didn't mind cleaning tables. There is no job that is beneath us in the Kingdom. If Jesus washed feet, then we have no room to refuse what God asks us to do. God has many plans in store for you, so don't judge a ministry opportunity too quickly. When we all serve willingly wherever God places us, we might start to see miracles as well!

Have you ever declined a chance to serve because it was "beneath you"? What was it? Would you respond the same way now?

Are you willing to do whatever God asks of you? Why or why not?

The Martyrdom of Saints
The Stoning of Stephen

memory verse

But Stephen, full of the Holy Spirit, looked up to heaven and saw the glory of God, and Jesus standing at the right hand of God. "Look," he said, "I see heaven open and the Son of Man standing at the right hand of God." **Acts 7:55-56**

Tertullian, a church leader in the second century, said, "The blood of the martyrs is the seed of the church." He was living through times of intense persecution, yet he saw the Church continue to grow and thrive. No matter how many Christians lost their lives, the Church continued to expand.

This kind of persecution began with the martyrdom of Stephen. A *martyr*, which means a *witness* in Greek, is someone who give his or her life for something he or she believes in. When faced with a crowd that wanted to destroy the fledgling Christian Church, Stephen gave bold witness to Jesus Christ. In reponse the enraged mob stoned him. His death wouldn't be the last, either. Throughout the history of the early Church, people gave their lives for the gospel: Stephen, James, Peter, Paul. Yet the Church continues to multiply again and again.

This kind of martyrdom does not just exist in the Bible. As you read this, people all over the world are still giving the ultimate sacrifice to spread the gospel of Christ. You and I may never be asked to make that sacrifice, but we will be asked to daily give our lives to Christ as we serve Him wherever He chooses to use us. This week we're going to ask the question, "Would I be willing to give my life for Christ?" Until we understand the sacrifice of past saints, we won't be able to follow in their footsteps today.

Day 1 >
Acts 7:54-60

Stephen gets credit for being the first Christian martyr. But why did he have to die? Jesus came to die, but that wasn't the end of His story. He endured the cross because He knew reality beyond this world exists. His ultimate goal is within that other reality, and that's where He wants us to set our goals. Stephen understood this and never asked "why?" His response to his coming death was almost identical to Christ's on the cross. When he saw Jesus it was a reminder that God was pleased with his actions and had everything under control. As we deal with persecution, we must remember there is more to life than what we now experience.

How does understanding our destination change the way we deal with pain and suffering here on earth?

Ask Jesus to show you how to live with your real future in mind.

Day 2 >>
Philippians 1:19-26

Paul made the ultimate sacrifice when he was murdered by Nero for his faith. But here we get a glimpse of his attitude about martyrdom. Paul had that long-term view we talked about yesterday and

community: The New Testament Church—The Essence of Fellowship

wanted to be with Christ. But he also knew that as long as he remained here he could serve the God he loved with his whole heart. Paul's goal was not simply a long life here; it was a productive life here. Ultimately he just wanted to be wherever God wanted him to be.

There is more to your life than simply living. Paul understood, as we should, that every minute we live surrendered to Christ benefits not only us, but everyone we come in contact with.

How would your life be different if you thought the way Paul did?

How are you using the time you've been given to help others know Christ?

Day 3 >>>
Acts 12:1-7

This is a confusing passage because it raises the question, "Why?" Why did God allow James to be killed yet send an angel to save Peter? Why does God allow anyone to die for his or her faith? We can't fully understand the answers to these questions now, but we can trust the character of the Father. God doesn't "play favorites," so He doesn't just save the lives of those He likes better. He has a plan that works out for the best and that plan has glory and paradise waiting for all of us who are in Him.

How we get there is up to God—not to us. We may not get the answers we want in understanding why things sometimes happen the way they do, but we can always trust God in spite of our circumstances.

When you are confused, where do you go for answers?

Do you go to God with your questions? Why or why not?

Spend some time talking to God about the things you don't understand about why things happen the way they do.

Day 4 >>>>
2 Timothy 1:8-12

In verse 12, Paul showed us another reason why he was not afraid to give his life for Jesus: He had given it up already. Paul was firmly convinced his old self had died when he became a believer and he had become a brand new person. That being the case, no one could take his life from him since he had given it up years ago. His new life was in Christ; therefore, whatever Christ asked him to do he would do. With this attitude Paul could walk through danger with confidence. In his mind he was already dead and his new life, which began at his conversion, was waiting for him after death. Knowing God is trustworthy gave him confidence to follow Jesus even to his own earthly death.

Have you given your whole life to Jesus? What parts have you kept back for yourself?

Are you convinced that God will take care of you no matter what?

Does your life reflect that?

Day 5 >>>>>
2 Timothy 4:6-8

Paul knew he would probably not return from Rome. He had been saved from death many times, but now the Lord had shown Him that this would be the end for Him. No one ever looks forward to his death, but Paul found comfort in this: He had done his best for the Lord. What an amazing thing to be able to say—that we have fought hard and kept our faith through it all. Paul was by no means perfect, but he had lived his life for Jesus and was prepared to lose his life for Him as well. Have you ever considered how you will finish? Will you be able to say the same thing Paul did when God asks you to finally come home?

If you were to die tomorrow, would you be pleased with your service to Christ?

Imagine what it will be like when God gives us a crown of glory for persevering in our faith.

God's Perfect Plan
The Dispersion of the Church

memory verse

Those who had been scattered preached the word wherever they went. **Acts 8:4**

Have you ever seen those Magic Eye pictures? You know, the ones that look like a bunch of jagged colors, but if you stare at them in a certain way a picture will leap out at you in 3D. I never could see the picture; in fact, all it did was give me a headache. But other people swear right in front of me in a bunch of chaos is an incredible picture. I have to say it's still hard to believe.

Sometimes, our lives will look like those pictures: completely random, jagged edges, and totally incomprehensible. But the Bible is very clear about the fact that even when things seem totally out of control, God has His firm hand on history. God is able at all times to work every circumstance for His purposes and His glory. In Acts 8:1-8, we see the early church face a huge wave of persecution. It looked bleak for the fledgling body of believers as they were scattered everywhere. But, this period of turmoil would serve to spread the gospel faster than anything else in the Book of Acts.

Even when we think nothing can be done, God can still do whatever He wishes in order to fix the situation. As we think about God's sovereignty this week, watch how He brings a perfect plan to fruition out of what looked like complete chaos.

Day 1 >

Acts 8:1-8

This could have been a bad day for the church. One of their leaders was killed by an angry mob and the believers were forced to flee to surrounding towns. To them it may have looked as if the church were on the brink of destruction. But in the very next verse we see what happened. God used this persecution to spread the message of Christ to more places. What was supposed to hurt the church actually made it grow larger and stronger! God knew this in advance. Sometimes He will allow things to happen that seem destructive. But rest assured He knows what's going on and will redeem all things for His purposes.

What are some things in your life you don't understand right now?

Ask God for the faith to trust Him even when things don't seem good.

Day 2 >>

Matthew 1:18-24

Have you ever thought about how crazy this sounds? It's positively insane. The whole goal of the Messiah coming was to liberate God's people and save them from their sins—and what we got was a baby. How was that supposed to work? It's questions like these that kept a lot of people from believing in Jesus while He was on earth. But this was God's plan from the beginning. Everyone had their own ideas about how the Messiah would save God's people, but no one saw that only through a perfect sacrifice could people be made whole. Our plans may seem grand and even God-honoring, but God's plans are what will stand because only His plans will work. God knows how to orchestrate everything for the best possible outcome, so we need to learn to trust His plans over ours—even when we'd like to choose the path ourselves.

Do you trust that God knows better than you how to run your life?

Who then makes the decisions about how you live?

Day 3 >>>
Exodus 13:17-14:18

"Are we lost?" I'm sure many were complaining as the Israelites began their wanderings. To them, it probably seemed as if someone was asleep at the wheel. They were taking a longer-than-needed route and then turned around to get trapped by the sea. But all of this was according to God's plan. None of them could have had in mind what God was planning for the Egyptians. Because Moses was firm in his resolve to follow God, we

have the record of one of the most stunning miracles in human history—the parting of the Red Sea. When God leads, He always has a reason—and a good one at that! Many times we want to grumble as the Israelites did that this isn't the right way to go. Instead, we should trust in God's sovereign hand to make things right even when we don't see how He'll do it.

If you had been one of the Israelites in this story, how would you have reacted?

Ask God to help you understand His sovereignty over your life and all creation.

Day 4 >>>>
Acts 9:10-19

Ananias was a random believer in Damascus. We don't read anything else about him in Scripture. Here he was asked to do a hard thing when God told him to pray for Saul. God might as well have asked him to put his head in a lion's mouth as far as Ananias was concerned. But God was insistent, so Ananias obeyed. This was Ananias' one moment to shine, and the consequences of his obedience have been shaking the whole world ever since. Never underestimate just one conversion. Human history changed when Saul was saved and adopted into the church ("Brother Saul," Ananias called him). You may think God's tasks for you are small, but never underestimate what God can do with one act of obedience.

Have you ever seen God use you in a way you didn't expect? How did that feel?

Spend today remembering that your actions can have eternal consequences. See what changes in your attitudes!

Day 5 >>>>>
Luke 18:31-34

One of God's enduring attributes is that He is a Redeemer. The word literally means one who "buys back." In Scripture it refers to how Jesus' blood paid for our sins. Here Jesus predicted His death and resurrection, and also the torture He would undergo beforehand. He knew this would happen— and chose to endure it anyway. One of the most barbaric acts in history brought the most glorious miracle of all: the salvation of our souls. That's redemption! God's ways can seem difficult and even wrong to us, but His sovereign plans are always redemptive no matter how bad it seems.

Spend some time thinking how God brought about so much good from something so horrible.

Ask God to help you see how He can always bring good out of circumstances, even evil circumstances.

An Amazing Conversion
Philip and the Ethiopian

memory verse

The eunuch was reading this passage of Scripture: "He was led like a sheep to the slaughter, and as a lamb before the shearer is silent, so he did not open his mouth."

Acts 8:32

Learning to drive is an interesting experience. Typically to learn to drive your parent or driving instructor will take you to some deserted road or parking lot to attempt your training. Driving seems like it should be easy—press the gas to go, use the wheel to turn—but a little more finesse is involved. After a few lurching starts and screeching halts, hopefully you start to get the hang of it. Or at least your instructor prays you do before he or she gets whiplash.

Learning new skills takes time. The disciples had to take some time to learn to walk in the Spirit. Having the Spirit of God present with them all the time meant amazing new opprotunities and an intimacy with God they had never experienced. The same can be true for us as we learn to walk in the Spirit. As with the first disciples, it will take some trial and error to work out the kinks.

This was certainly true for Philip, one of the seven chosen to help the apostles. This week we're going to learn how the Spirit worked within the encounter between Philip and the Ethiopian. Each day we'll tackle a different aspect of the story and pick ways we can learn how to respond to the Holy Spirit in our lives. You never know: by the end of the week you might end up being a part of a similarly amazing story.

Day 1 >
Acts 8:26-40

I don't know about you, but I'd love it if God talked to me like this all the time. In the first three verses of this story, God spoke twice to Philip in complete sentences with specific instructions. Sign me up for that! But does the Spirit really speak that way today? Well, yes and no. Sometimes God has very specific things for us to do and will be very direct in letting us know. You may find yourself in a spot where you know without a doubt that God wants you to do something right now. The Spirit doesn't usually speak this way, but when He does we need to be obedient as Philip was and take advantage of whatever opportunity God is providing.

Have you ever experienced God speaking to you like this?

How did you know it was Him?

Ask God to help you hear His voice when He is speaking to you.

Day 2 >>
Acts 8:30-31

God didn't decide to just throw Philip at the Ethiopian to see how he'd do. Instead, God sent him into a prepared situation. God had already been working in the Ethiopian's life and now He wanted to use Philip to seal the deal. God uses us in similar ways. When He asks you to do something, He isn't just asking on a whim; He has a reason for it. God always prepares our way. When we know this, it takes a lot of the fear out of following God. No matter how odd it may seem, God has a plan when He asks us to serve in a particular way. Always remember that you are a part of a much larger plan.

How do you think God might be moving in the lives of people around you right now?

Is He asking you to help them in any way?

Ask God to show you clearly what to do.

Day 3 >>>
Acts 8:31-35

How do you know when the Spirit is involved in something? Listen to Scripture. Here the Ethiopian was reading a passage that includes a Messianic prophecy. It's a passage in the Old Testament talking about Jesus. Philip immediately knew that the Spirit was leading this man through the Word and explained that to him. Since the Spirit inspired the Bible, He will often use it to keep us grounded, teach us new things, and point others to Jesus. It is possible to misuse Scripture, but if we are familiar with the Word we should be able to recognize the real thing when we hear it. Staying in touch with Scripture is one the best ways to accurately hear the voice of the Spirit.

Has the Spirit ever taught you something through Scripture?

What was it?

Ask the Father to show you how to use Scripture to help others around you.

Day 4 >>>>
Acts 8:34-38

The Spirit began this story with hands-on involvement by telling Philip exactly where to go. Notice, however, that the story ends with Philip handling the situation. I'm sure Philip was walking in the Spirit as he explained the gospel to the Ethiopian, but Philip still did the talking. When we follow God, His intention is not for us to become robots He can use at a moment's notice. We don't get possessed by the Spirit. Instead, He points us in the right direction and enables us to accomplish the goal. He wants to involve us, not just use us. That's how we act as mature sons and daughters of God—not just infants in Christ.

If God pointed you in the right direction, would you be willing to walk with Him into the task?

Look around today and see if there is any place where God might be pushing you to serve.

Day 5 >>>>>
Acts 8:36-39

Why was the Ethiopian so ready to be baptized? Because he knew he had been changed. We've already seen how the Spirit came in the form of fire on the apostles at Pentecost—marking them with the Spirit. For us it's a little different. When you got saved you may not have seen any tongues of fire falling on your head but the Spirit rushed in nonetheless. When you get baptized, you are having your own celebration of Pentecost moment. It's a symbolic act where we recognize that the Holy Spirit has changed us; we have been given new power just like the first disciples. The Ethiopian didn't get fire, but he saw the water. If baptism seems boring to you, try to look past the actual water and see the fire that is represented—the fire of the Spirit changing a person's life forever!

How has your life changed since you became a Christian?

How does it feel to know that what happened to the apostles is happening to you?

The Apostle to the Gentiles
The Conversion of Saul

memory verse

He fell to the ground and heard a voice say to him, "Saul, Saul, why do you persecute me?" "Who are you, Lord?" Saul asked. "I am Jesus, whom you are persecuting," he replied. "Now get up and go into the city, and you will be told what you must do." **Acts 9:4-6**

You can't talk about the New Testament without talking about Paul. In fact, Christianity itself would not be the same without the life, writings, and influence of the apostle to the Gentiles. Something happened in the life of this one man that served as a turning point in history. Acts 9:1-19 records the amazing conversion of this great man—literally the transformation from "Saul the zealous Jew" to "Paul the crusader for Christ."

Paul's influence literally cannot be measured. Fulfilling His will from the beginning, God chose Paul to be His vessel to take the message of salvation to everyone—not just the Jews. Paul was the first missionary to the rest of us. Furthermore, God inspired Paul in his writings. He ultimately left behind thirteen letters in our recorded Scriptures.

Part average-Joe, part fierce debater, and part loving pastor, Paul's unique character and background made him the perfect choice as the apostle to everyone.

As you read the Book of Acts, you see the depth of conviction of this persecutor turned true believer. And he's everywhere: in the marketplace talking to ordinary folks, in the synagogue debating religious leaders, and on the road spreading the gospel from Asia to Europe. This week, we're going to look at the conversion of the church's first and greatest theologian and find out why God is still using Paul in our lives today.

Acts 9:1-19

This is one of the most famous stories in the Bible. In fact, it shows up three times just in the Book of Acts (see chapters 21 and 26). Why so often? This was Paul's defining moment when his whole life changed. Before this point, Paul thought he was working for God and found out he was doing the opposite. But the great thing is that God came to him anyway. Paul knew that God loved him, had forgiven him, and was sending him on a mission of great importance. He knew it would cause him pain and probably cost him his life, but it was worth it to serve a God who could love a sinner like him.

What was your conversion like?

How has it changed your life?

Who have you told your conversion story to lately?

Ask God to show you where you could share your story with someone this week.

Day 2 >>

1 Corinthians 1:1-3, 9

I was always confused when people said they had a "calling from God." I didn't doubt them, because Paul obviously had a calling as we read yesterday. He even used the phrase "called to be an apostle." But notice that we also have a general calling. In verse 2 Paul reminds us that all of us as believers have a calling from God to be pure. We should be pursuing the calling we have already received. But will God ever call you as He called Paul? Maybe. Callings are very unique and God uses a variety of ways to help each of us understand His specific will. Don't look for Paul's experience, though; look for God's work specifically in your own life.

Do you feel that God may be calling you to some form of specific service?

Ask God to make that calling clear to you. Talk to your pastor or another respected Christian leader for guidance.

Day 3 >>>
Philippians 3:3-11

If you looked at Paul from a religious perspective you'd see the perfect minister. Any Jew of that day would have envied Paul and probably assumed he was a very holy man just by his pedigree. It would be the equivalent today of growing up in church, having Billy Graham for your dad, getting straight A's in seminary, never getting into trouble, and always knowing the right church answers. Paul basically had the equivalent of that going for him,

but he saw all of it as useless. In other words, none of that stuff changed him. It was his personal relationship with Jesus that mattered, not his polished reputation. Anyone can think you're holy, but what matters is that you really know Jesus.

Read verses 7-10 again. Try to understand Paul's heart as he wrote that.

Do you feel the way Paul felt?

Ask God to help you truly know Him.

Day 4 >>>>
2 Corinthians 10:10;
1 Corinthians 2:1-5

We don't know what Paul looked like. From the amazing impact he had on so many people, it is tempting to imagine him as a dashing charismatic figure. But the clues in Scripture say otherwise. Paul was most likely not very attractive and he wasn't even the best communicator. Many speakers of that day dressed well and gave incredibly entertaining speeches. Paul was criticized for not being more like them. Paul wasn't interested in entertainment; he was interested in the power of God. Who do you listen to? If you only listen to those who entertain you, you might hear an interesting speech, but you will miss out on people like Paul—and that's where the real spiritual power is.

Spend some time reflecting on where God is moving around you.

Could God be moving you in unexpected ways?

Keep your eyes open for God to speak to you through anyone or anything today, not just in the places you'd expect.

Day 5 >>>>>
Philippians 3:12-14

It's tempting to put our leaders on pedestals. They can do more than we can, so we tend to idolize them. Because of that we can also look down on ourselves. Paul knew that the Philippians might begin thinking more of him than they should, so here he reminded them that he too was growing in Christ. Our mentors and leaders aren't better than us; they've just had more time to work at it than we have. Each of us will be able to know God as well as they do if were diligent as they have been. They aren't superhuman; they're just committed. God uses them as role models to show us that it can be done. If we follow in their footsteps, we'll see the same power and joy in our lives.

How are you pressing on to be like Christ?

Thank God today for the spiritual leaders He's put in your life to show you the way.

From Jews to Gentiles
Peter and Cornelius

memory verse

We are witnesses of everything he did in the country of the Jews and in Jerusalem. They killed him by hanging him on a tree, but God raised him from the dead on the third day and caused him to be seen. **Acts 10:39-40**

It's hard for me to believe people once thought the earth was flat, or that it was the center of the universe. Imagine you had believed all your life that the earth was flat. How much would it have changed your reality if someone told you the world was big ball circling a gigantic star and that all those tiny pinpricks in the night sky are stars hundreds of times bigger than the earth?

I imagine the Jews in Acts felt the same type of reality change when they found out that God wasn't just interested in them, but wanted to save the whole world. They saw themselves as "the chosen people," but now God was calling them to open the doors to allow non-Jews to receive salvation in Jesus Christ.

In Acts 10 we find that God gave Peter a specific vision to make him realize that salvation was for all people, not just the Jews. The result of this revelation was an explosion of evangelism that quickly moved beyond Israel's borders and began to echo around the world. That shockwave is still expanding as the gospel is shared with people who have never heard it.

Some people say the gospel is too exclusive since it requires belief in Jesus. The gospel is one of the most inclusive of all faiths since it is open to anyone who will believe. This week we will look at the heart of God and His message of love and peace. We'll also see where we fit into His plan as He sends His gospel to all the nations.

Day 1 >

Acts 10:9-48

You have to give God credit for being dramatic. But why all the theatrics here? Because this event was a big turning point for Peter—and for Christianity. Peter had followed the Law, and as far as he understood it there were things you could and couldn't eat. The same was true for people: some were considered to be God's people and some were not. In simple terms, Jews were and everyone else wasn't. So God started with something less important (food) and then moved to something very important (people) to help Peter understand. And Peter got the message: God loves all people—not just the Jews—and wants all of them to be His people. Peter resisted this thought at first. But it was unmistakable what God was telling Him, so he changed his mind. God's love is for all people, not just a chosen few.

How would you have reacted if God asked you to change your mind about something you've always believed?

Is there any place in your life where you believe some people are more important than others? Why?

How does this passage help you deal with that?

community: The New Testament Church—The Essence of Fellowship

Day 2 >>

Genesis 12:1-3

Peter probably thought that God's openness to the Gentiles was new, but God had wanted this from the beginning. Abraham was the father of the Jewish people. (Remember the children's song, "Father Abraham"?) God told Abraham he would father a nation. His children would be special—God's people. But look at today's passage. God told Abraham His desire: that "all peoples on earth will be blessed through you." This was God's plan all along, that everyone could be blessed and have a relationship with God.

If God loves everyone, how should you treat people outside your race, color, or national background?

Pray that God will help you realize that all people are God's people and that the biggest difference is that some are lost and some are saved.

Day 3 >>>

1 John 2:1-3

Humans are rather diverse. We have different languages, heritages, customs, and appearances. We live in different environments. But there is one thing we all share in common: our sin nature. It affects everyone, and in that respect it is the great equalizer. No one can say he is without sin and no one can overcome it by his own effort. John reminded believers to remember where they came from (they used to be lost in sin) and to keep doors open for others. Jesus came to save people who are struggling with sin. That includes everyone. If we are going to be the Church of Jesus Christ, our doors have to remain open to everyone.

Now that you're saved, do you tend to look down on people who aren't?

Ask Jesus to show you how to love all people, not just those you love now.

Day 4 >>>>>
Jonah 3:3-4:4

Most of us know about Jonah's aquatic adventures (see Jonah 1-2), but here we find the rest of the story. When Jonah finally obeyed God and preached to the Ninevites, they changed their ways. Instead of being thrilled, Jonah pouted. He hated the Ninevites and would rather have seen them destroyed. Again, here we have an Old Testament example of God's compassion for all people, even a brutal race like the Ninevites.

Prejudice has no place in the church because it has no place in the heart of God. If God can forgive all people, then

we must as well. But if prophets can suffer from prejudice, so can we.

If God told you to share his love with someone you really despised, could you do it?

Ask God to change your heart so that you can love people like He does.

Day 5 >>>>>
Acts 1:6-8

God could have sent Jesus to every part of the world to tell them about salvation, but instead He chose to send you! Part of our job as the church is to take the message of Jesus to all those who have not heard it. There are over one billion people on the planet today who literally have no idea who Jesus is. They have no hope that they can be saved from their own sin. God is sending us out—just as He sent the first disciples—to share the good news with a lost world. He loves them and desperately wants them to know salvation. If this is God's heart, it should be ours as well.

Have you felt God calling you to share the gospel with people outside your culture?

How can you do that this week . . . this month . . . this year?

Ask God to show you where He wants to use you.

A Growing Church
The Church at Antioch

memory verse

The Lord's hand was with them, and a great number of people believed and turned to the Lord.
Acts 11:21

I don't know about you, but I am continually amazed at how fast babies grow. You see them one month and they are small and helpless, then just a few months later they're walking, talking, and generally creating havoc wherever they go. Amazing.

Most of us have stopped growing so maybe we don't appreciate this as much. I'm sure God meant for babies to stop growing at a certain point, but not the church.

In Acts 11:19-26, we see the Church multiplying and growing exponentially as the gospel moved into new areas. This growth was explosive as the Church tore down the barriers of cultural prejudice, geographical isolation, racial division, and social opposition. This is what God desires for His Kingdom—continually expanding and bringing more people into the knowledge of Christ.

The same Holy Spirit who inspired this expansion is continuing to work in us today. Many of the barriers faced by the early Church members still threaten us, but they can be torn down just as easily through His power. This week we're going to find out that God wants to use us to reach the world by multiplying the number of believers in our churches.

Day 1 >
Acts 11:19-26

Since we've never lived in Israel, place-names can all run together. But the Bible records them for a reason. Antioch wasn't in Israel; it was in Syria. It was filled with Gentiles, not Jews. The gospel was bursting past the borders of ancient Israel and beginning to spread to the rest of the world.

All of a sudden the make-up of the church was becoming remarkably diverse. There were people of all kinds coming into the church—so many that they were becoming a totally new entity. And once their numbers became large enough, people invented a name for them . . . a name you and I now share along with these early followers of Christ: Christian.

How do you react when people who are very different from you join your church?

Do people in your school see a difference between Christians and non-Christians?

Do your actions help show that Christians are different? How?

Day 2 >>
John 4:21-26

Jews and Samaritans didn't get along. Although the Samaritans were descendents of Jews, they had intermarried with pagan peoples and were considered half-breeds and not true Jews.. But in today's Scripture passage, Jesus showed how the gospel overcomes such barriers. Jesus was ready to share the good news with people that other Jews wouldn't associate with. In Acts 8, we've already seen Philip going to this region to share Jesus' resurrection.

If we are going to see the gospel spread, we have to tear down the boundaries that separate us from others. In our country factors such as race, social and economic status, and different religious beliefs sometimes keep us isolated. But as believers, we have to be willing to cross those barriers for the sake of the gospel.

What is the hardest barrier for you to overcome in sharing your faith?

Ask Jesus to help you overcome these barriers for the sake of the gospel.

Day 3 >>>
Matthew 5:13-16

No matter what your spiritual gifts are, all of us are called to share Christ with others. Some of us may be better at it than others, but each Christian has this responsibility. Are you willing to do your part? Unless we make witnessing a core value of our lives, we will probably be distracted and never get around to witnessing to

community: The New Testament Church—The Essence of Fellowship

people. It's easy enough to let other people share their faith, but God wants all of us to be committed to bringing people to Christ. If the church grows, it will be because each of us is sharing our faith.

Spend some time thinking about why it is so important to share your faith.

Then think about some ways you can begin reaching out to the people for whom you have a burden. Write some ideas for doing so here.

If you do not have this burden, ask God to give it to you.

Day 4 >>>>
Acts 13:1-5

Over the course of his ministry, Paul went on three missionary journeys and covered thousands of miles sharing the gospel. He wanted the message of salvation to reach as many people as possible, and he didn't mind making a long trip to accomplish that goal. How about you? God may call you to go on a short-term mission trip or even to spend a summer away from home so you can share the gospel with others who do not know Christ. There is a lot of work to be done at home, but God's call to all of us is to take His good news to the ends of the earth. If believers don't go, that goal will not be accomplished.

Pray about whether God wants to use you in mission work in the near future.

Pray for those who, like Paul, are right now taking the gospel to new places.

Day 5 >>>>>

1 Corinthians 5:9-10

The Corinthians had misinterpreted Paul's advice, so he had to set them straight. Apparently they had lots of fellowship with other Christians, but no meaningful contact with lost people. (Sounds like churches today.) In the church, we must keep each other accountable; but sometimes churches become so self-focused that non-Christians won't come near them. God intends for us to be out among the people of the world so they can see the difference in our lives. And if we're going to be effective, this needs to be up close and personal. Don't try to do this alone. All believers need to act as one to interact with a lost and dying world. Otherwise, all our salt will end up back in the saltshaker on Sundays but have no real impact on the world on a day-to-day basis.

Do you have any contact with non-believers? Who?

Ask the Father to show you how to build positive and meaningful relationships with the lost people in your world with whom you come in contact.

community: The New Testament Church—The Essence of Fellowship

Reaching the Lost
Paul's First Missionary Journey

memory verse

While they were worshiping the Lord and fasting, the Holy Spirit said, "Set apart for me Barnabas and Saul for the work to which I have called them." So after they had fasted and prayed, they placed their hands on them and sent them off.
Acts 13:2-3

If you've never been outside of the United States, it is tempting to assume that everyone around the world lives kind of like you do. My first mission trip to Mexico cured me of that delusion. I had the privilege of helping build small houses for people who literally lived in huts made out of garbage. Until then I had never thought about the needs of those who lived so far away from my day-to-day existence. But once I saw their needs, I could never forget. Even though their physical needs were striking, they had deeper needs than the physical ones.

This week we see God sending missionaries out to reach a lost world as Paul embarked on his first missionary journey. Some pretty amazing things happened on this trip. But the most important thing was that the message of Christ was preached to people who had probably never heard it before. The influence of the gospel was beginning to be felt outside of Judea, Galilee, and Samaria.

God never forgets about the needs of the lost and desires for them all to come to faith in Christ. In order to accomplish that goal He is sending us—all of us. No matter who we are or what our spiritual gifts are, all of us are to be involved in reaching the lost with the message of Jesus Christ. Until those needs are met, we all have a job to do. So pack your bags; it's time to get going.

Day 1 >

Acts 13:1-12

In order to spread the gospel to people who had never heard, missionaries had to be sent out. Paul and Barnabas were chosen to go. In today's passage, Paul and Barnabas reach out to a Roman official, so already we see them pressing beyond the bounds of the Jewish believers. In order to reach the lost we will have to go to those outside our normal routine. That may scare you. Who knows what might happen? You're right. But what might happen is that many people could be saved—just as we see in this passage. Until we are willing to go wherever God wants, we probably won't go anywhere. We won't see any miracles either. God is calling us all to go in some way, which means we can't stay where we are doing what we're doing unless we are doing what He wants us to.

If God called you to go and serve Him in a distant land for a time, do you think you could go?

Ask the Father to show you how to be open to going out to serve Him.

Day 2 >>

Acts 13:1-3

Let's think about this passage from another perspective. How would it feel to have to send two of your friends to preach to others? While the church must have been excited about the prospect of more people coming to faith in Jesus, they were also losing the constant presence of these ministers in their lives. One of the ways we participate in missions is sacrificing our personal gain for the sake of the lost. God will call people from our congregations to spread the gospel in other lands. Our job is to send them and support their missionary work. It's not only a sacrifice for the missionaries but for us as well.

Are you willing to personally sacrifice for the sake of those who don't know Jesus?

Ask the Lord God to give you a sacrificial heart today.

Day 3 >>>
Colossians 4:2-6; 2 Thessalonians 3:1-2

Not all of us are called to full-time mission work. But whether we actually cross the borders of another country or not, we can still have a powerful impact on world missions. Here, Paul prayed for help knowing that the prayers of his home churches were extremely important. While in prison it was a great encouragement to know he wasn't alone on the mission field, but was instead surrounded by the prayers of his friends back home. All of us at home need to pray for the safety and effectiveness of our missionaries abroad. In this way all of us are involved in God's plans for the nations. Think about it . . . when you pray, those prayers immediately impact missionaries and lost people around the world.

Are any missionaries from your church?

Find out . . . And if there are, spend some time praying for them each day this week. If there are not, get a list of missionaries who have birthdays on each day this week and pray for them.

Day 4 >>>>

Matthew 9:35-38

You don't have to go far to answer the call to reach the lost. Here Jesus sees a multitude of ministry opportunities right in his home nation of Israel. Today there are thousands of ministry opportunities right in our own nation—even in your hometown. Jesus described his home turf as a field ripe for harvest for anyone willing to do the work. Look around today. You interact with people daily who need to hear about Jesus. Try praying today for those who stand in line with you, those you see at restaurants, and those you go to school or work with. It could be that the greatest missions opportunity is right in front of you.

How can you reach out to those you see on a regular basis—but don't really know?

Pray earnestly that God would use you right where you are to tell others about Jesus.

Day 5 >>>>>
Matthew 28:18-20; Romans 10:14-15

God's command to all of us is to go and make disciples of *all nations*. Someone must go to those nations because right now millions have never heard the name of Jesus. The Great Commission applies to all of us, so we all have a call to missions. God will call some of us to go, some of us to pray for those He sends, and some of us to give financially from our abundance in order to meet their needs. But regardless of what our role is, we are all called to help those nations hear the good news about Jesus. The trap we must avoid is assuming that missions is someone else's job. If no one actually goes to tell them, they will never be saved. Is God asking you to go to those who have never heard His name?

Ask one of your pastors about missions opportunities for you—both now and in the future. See what various kinds of missions work is available.

Ask the Father today how He wants you to be involved in missions.

Supporting Missionaries
Paul and Barnabas Return to Antioch

memory verse

Paul and Barnabas appointed elders for them in each church and, with prayer and fasting, committed them to the Lord, in whom they had put their trust. **Acts 14:23**

Before the lofty days of digital photography and fancy computer programs, we had slide projectors. On Sunday nights when I was a kid, missionaries would come home and give us a slide show about where they had been and what the Lord had done in their ministry. You cannot possibly imagine how boring this was to me. I wanted amazing stories of angels, narrow escapes, and exorcisms, but they never came. Just stories of people being saved, lives changed, and communities transformed by the love of Jesus. Of course, I had totally missed the point. They weren't flashy, but those missionaries were literally the heroes of the faith standing before me. These people had left all the cushy comforts of home and traded them for a chance to serve Christ on the front lines by sharing the gospel. And while they may not have wowed me with their presentations, their spiritual impact was tremendous.

In Acts, Paul and Barnabas came home from their mission trip to give their version of a slide show. Supporting the missionaries who come to your church may not be your top priority, but it is Jesus'. This week we're going to see how we can support those who are called away even when we're not.

Day 1 >
Acts 14:21-28

If you've been away for a while, it's always good to come home. The mission field is exciting and rewarding, but also turbulent and tiring. Paul may have seemed like a vagabond as he went from place to place, but he knew where his home was and promptly returned there at the end of this first missionary journey. Imagine coming home after being away for over a year, and you can understand how he must have felt.

Maintaining the home base is one of the ways we support our missionaries, reminding them again and again that though they may sometimes feel alone on the field, we are always supporting them. You may not know their names, but they need you nonetheless.

Is your church a home to you? How can you build relationships so it becomes one?

Pray for those in your church serving Christ away from your church home.

Day 2 >>
Acts 14:27-28

Remember, there were no pictures back then, no video, no Internet. These people never really saw a lot outside their hometown. For Paul to tell them about what God was doing in another land was like news from another planet. Letters had been their only real correspondence since Paul left. So getting a chance to hear what God was doing in other places was a rare privilege. Sometimes we can take for granted our ability to instantly see what is going on in other places. We see and hear so much that we become calloused to what is truly exciting. If we are not interested in how God is moving around the world, maybe we've gotten too caught up in the world we live in.

What are some of the most exciting things to you? Are they eternal or temporary?

Ask the Lord to give you a hunger to know how He is moving around the world.

Day 3 >>>
Ephesians 4:1-13

Let's be honest. For many of us the idea of doing mission work is another country has never appealed to us. And the truth is, not all of us will be called to go. The mistake we can make is to assume that if we aren't called to go we don't have to do anything. But in this passage Paul reminds us that although we are given different gifts, the goal is that we all be unified and grow into maturity. Unless each of us uses our different gifts, this won't happen. Translation: Unless we support those who have different callings than ours, we'll never grow to fullness in Christ. So even if mission work isn't your thing, we still need to be actively involved in supporting those who do have that calling.

How can you begin to regularly support missionaries?

Think about those with different callings than yours. Thank God for giving them this gift and pray for their continued growth.

Day 4 >>>>
1 Corinthians 9:7-15

Not all the churches were spiritually minded. Paul chided the Corinthians for not supporting missionaries. Although he wasn't asking them to support him, he was reminding them that they received great benefit when other churches originally sent Paul and Barnabas to them. In like manner they should bless others by supporting more missionaries. If supporting missionaries or taking time to pray for them ever seems to be a burden to you, think back to all the people God has sent to help you grow. Sunday School teachers, pastors, camp counselors, youth ministers . . . and all of these individuals were supported by someone else so they could help you. Shouldn't we do the same for others?

Have you ever had an attitude like the Corinthians?

How can we avoid this mentality?

Spend some time thanking God today for the people He has used in your life. Thank them today personally if possible.

Day 5 >>>>>
Acts 14:27-28

Put yourself in the shoes of Joe Worshipper from Antioch. A while back they asked for an offering to help this guy named Paul. You were new to the church and didn't know the guy, but in obedience to Christ you decided to give some money to help his ministry. Later he returned and began telling you that the gospel is going farther than it ever has. Churches were started in cities that before had none. And thousands had come to faith in Christ. He looked at you and said thank you for supporting him. Who knew that a small act of obedience could have such far-reaching results? This very scenario is played out every time we support mission-aries with money, love, and prayers.

Find out if any missionaries are serving that have come from your church. If so, get in contact with them and find out how you can support them. If there are no missionaries serving from your church, ask your pastor or youth pastor to help you find some you can get in touch with.

Healing a Rift
The Jerusalem Council

memory verse

God, who knows the heart, showed that he accepted them by giving the Holy Spirit to them, just as he did to us. He made no distinction between us and them, for he purified their hearts by faith.
Acts 15:8-9

It's hard to love people on the other side. From a football rival to your nation's sworn enemy, it's hard to love anyone who isn't on your side—for whatever reason. The tension between groups can grow from a minor rivalry to anger, hatred, and even violence that can be sustained for centuries. This was the case for the Jews and Gentiles. The Jews were called by God to be His chosen people. Everyone else wasn't. Gentiles, the name given to any non-Jew, were typically excluded from most Jewish ceremonies and were considered unclean.

So imagine the surprise of the Jewish Christians when Gentiles began receiving the same Holy Spirit they had received. "You mean God loves them, too?" Paul and Peter had begun ministries to bring Gentiles into the new church. But with the inclusion of Gentiles came a huge problem for the Jews: "How do we get along with the people we've always excluded?" In Acts 15, we even have a record of a pretty heated discussion between Paul, Barnabas, Peter, James, and other apostles and elders of the church concerning this problem.

This week we're going to look at how the early church responded to God's call to love all people, not just the ones they were comfortable with. The challenge for the Jewish Christians is our challenge today as God calls us to love and include everyone— even the ones we see as being on the "other side."

Day 1 >

Acts 15:6-12; 22-30

This could have been a disaster. Strong opinions were held on both sides, as the Jewish Christians had to decide how to treat their new Gentile brothers and sisters. In the end the leaders decided that no matter what they thought before, they had to follow where God led. Conflict is inevitable in our lives since God is continually helping us grow and change from what we are to what we need to be. In order to resolve conflict we have to be willing to change even the things we hold dear if God asks us to. These leaders were humble and open to the movement of God; therefore, a crisis was averted. Are you as willing to change if God asks?

What are some of the subjects God has changed your mind about?

Are you willing to obey even if you don't get your way? Why or why not?

Ask God help you to apply today's Scripture passage to your own life.

Day 2 >>

Ephesians 2:11-22

In the Temple there were signs on a low wall that literally warned Gentiles that if they crossed that line they would be killed—

community: The New Testament Church—The Essence of Fellowship

immediately. And they meant it. When God revealed His plan to extend salvation to their hated rivals, the Jewish Christians probably wondered why. But here Paul explains: God wants a unified family. God doesn't want a bunch of isolated pockets of believers; He wants us to join together in Him. The point of breaking down dividing walls isn't just for the sake of breaking them down, but making us into the amazingly powerful Kingdom He wants us to be. We can't do that on our own. We need each other. We become who we are meant to be when we follow Christ . . . together.

Read the passage again and try to put yourself in the shoes of both the Jews and Gentiles.

What will it take to join with believers you normally don't associate with?

Pray for guidance for God's help.

Day 3 >>>
Ephesians 3:1-11

Why is it so important that we love those outside our comfort zone? In verse 9 of today's passage Paul told us that unifying across the barriers that divide us sends a message to the rest of the world that God is at work. Even more amazing, Paul said that it sends this message to all heavenly beings, not just humans. God is doing something in us that has never been done before. It's so new that even the heavenly hosts are shocked to see how God could bring such different groups of people together in Christ. It's not easy, but the impact of our unity has cosmic proportions. Have you ever imagined how important your actions are in the grand scheme of things?

If you knew your actions had cosmic impact, how would it change your priorities and choices?

Who can you reach out to today who is outside your comfort zone?

Day 4 >>>>
Galatians 2:11-14

Change doesn't always stick. In yesterday's Scripture we saw how Peter made the right call by standing up for Gentile believers. But here he was slipping back into his old ways. Paul rightfully challenged him to return to the right path. Sometimes people know the right decision but still make a bad choice. They may need us to help them stand firm when they are pressured to backslide. Peter and Paul were friends and partners in sharing the gospel. Are you willing to do the same for your friends when they backslide? We aren't the Holy Spirit, but we are called to help one another stay on track when times are tough.

Has anyone ever confronted you about something you did? How did you respond?

Is God asking you to help a friend stay on the path right now?

How can you do that in a loving manner?

Day 5 >>>>>
Colossians 3:12-14

Sometimes it's hard to move beyond old anger. Whether someone hurt you or maybe you just never got along, it's just not as easy as shaking hands and being friends. God doesn't expect you to just pretend that there's no past between you and old enemies, but He does expect you to forgive and move toward unity. Even if it takes time, we should be committed to allowing old wounds to heal so we can be unified as believers in Christ. Let go of the grudges, stop bringing up the past, and give someone another chance. Over time, God will heal the old wounds and replace them with unity among people who are really Christians.

Is there any past history that is building a wall between you and another believer?

What would it take for you to begin moving on from that hurt?

Ask the Father to help you begin to heal.

Valuable for Service
Paul and Barnabas' Disagreement

memory verse

Some time later Paul said to Barnabas, "Let us go back and visit the brothers in all the towns where we preached the word of the Lord and see how they are doing." **Acts 15:36**

There are a few misconceptions about the Christian life we ought to clear up right away. Misconception #1: *Pastors don't sin. They're perfect and should be expected never to fail.* While most pastors are great people and should be held to a high standard, they do sin and do fail. And if you expect them to be perfect, you're going to be disappointed. Misconception #2: *Real Christians always get along and never have fights.* In a perfect world . . . maybe. But we do not live in a perfect world. Even though two Christians may be sincerely trying their best to walk with Christ, they can still have conflicts with each another. It's just one of those pesky consequences of not being perfect.

Thankfully, the Bible doesn't whitewash conflicts between believers, even when they involve our most respected leaders. Acts 15 records one of these altercations between Paul and his friend Barnabus over yet another leader, young John Mark.

Whether we like it or not, we're going to have to deal with conflict—and not just with unbelievers, but with our brothers and sisters in Christ, too. It's hard and uncomfortable, but if we choose to look to Christ for help and not allow our feelings to guide us, we can usually find a godly compromise. This week we're going to look at how Paul and Barnabas responded to each other and how they ultimately resolved their conflict. Hopefully, we'll gain some insight into how we can handle conflict in our lives as well.

Day 1 >
Acts 15:36-40

I thought that if you were really following God you'd never have any disagreements. Umm, no. Even when we are seeking God sincerely, we can still be wrong— or at the very least we can fail to see the best path to take. Even though Paul and Barnabas were friends and were involved in an amazing ministry, this disagreement drove them apart. Conflict will occur in all relationships—even with your best friends. When this happens you sometimes have to be willing to leave your own desires and selfishness at the door and ask God to guide you. Then you must follow God as best you know, even if it means parting company for a while.

How do you deal with conflict?

Do you ask God for guidance or do you simply do whatever you feel?

Ask God to be the mediator of your conflicts with others.

Day 2 >>
2 Timothy 4:9-12

Whatever grievance he had against John Mark in the past, Paul had forgiven him and moved on. People—even those we love and care about—are going to let us down in this life, but we can't just write people off when they fail us. If we do, we will miss out on what God is doing in their lives and the blessings He wants to bring us through them. Paul was willing to look past old hurts and allow forgiveness to heal their friendship. He also recognized that John Mark was a fine leader and that his past history shouldn't keep them from working together.

Has someone ever let you down big-time? When?

Did you mend your friendship with that person?

If not, are you willing to allow God to heal your relationship with that person in the same way Paul did with John Mark?

Ask the Father to help you forgive those who have let you down.

Day 3 >>>
John 21:15-19

Peter made a lot of mistakes. He was brash. He talked when he should've been quiet. Right before this incident, he had denied Jesus three times. Not the picture of the most qualified person to lead the early church. Yet Jesus knew that in time Peter would make it. Jesus was able to look beyond Peter's faults to see the leader that

Peter was becoming. We can avoid a lot of conflicts in our relationships when we are able to have patience with others' mistakes. And if you ever get tired of putting up with their failures, remember they are doing the same for you!

Ask God today for patience in dealing with people whom you may not get along with.

Spend some time praying for them and your attitude towards them.

Day 4 >>>>
1 Peter 5:13-14

We're pretty familiar with John Mark by now, but you may actually be more familiar with him than you know. While John Mark initially offended Peter and went on his own way for a while, he ultimately became a very influential member of the church. Here we find him serving with Peter. Tradition tells us that John Mark is the author of the Gospel of Mark. But if he wasn't a disciple, how did he find out about what Jesus said and did? From Peter. Even though he made some relational mistakes early in his ministry, God still had huge plans for this young man—plans that have been helping believers for two thousand years. Never underestimate what God can do with willing hearts—even those who have made mistakes in the past.

Could God use you like He used John Mark? Why or why not?

Ask God to help you learn from your mistakes so you can continue to serve Him wherever He sends you.

Day 5 >>>>>
Colossians 4:10-11

Here we see an incident several years after our passage on Day 1. John Mark was now serving Paul while he was in jail in Rome. Everyone makes mistakes, but even this doesn't disqualify you from ministry. John Mark had chosen to abandon Paul earlier in his life, but here he was serving with him again. Like John Mark, we cannot let past failures hinder us from learning from our mistakes, repenting, and growing as Christians. John Mark was willing to make amends with Paul and join him again in ministry. Conflicts will occur, but resolution is always possible if both parties are willing to forgive and move on. Don't let embarrassment over past failures keep you from enjoying a godly friendship.

Have you ever done something that you felt disqualified you from being used by God?

Have you repented and gotten back on track?

You can! Ask God now to help you do that.

Spiritual Parenthood
Paul's 2nd Missionary Journey and Timothy

So the churches were strengthened in the faith and grew daily in numbers. **Acts 16:5**

Babies require a lot of attention . . . in the morning, in the afternoon, and at night. If you don't believe me, ask a new parent at your church.

Spiritual babies are the same: they require a lot of attention. When people come to faith in Christ, they don't wake up the next morning with all the answers. In fact, it's the questions of new believers that keep multiplying. So it's a good thing there are mature Christians around to help them.

In addition to our biological parents, God provides spiritual parents to show us how to grow in Christ. Your spiritual parent may be your pastor, youth minister, or a good Christian friend. Spiritual parents are crucial to your spiritual growth.

Paul played this role for a young man named Timothy. In Acts 16, Paul, already on his second missionary journey, decided to bring Timothy along. Paul basically spent the rest of his life mentoring Timothy. Paul became

Timothy's spiritual parent and helped him mature in the faith.

As you grow spiritually, God desires for you to parent other young believers. In fact, you should always have at least two people in your life: someone who is discipling you (a "Paul") and someone you are discipling (a "Timothy"). This week we're going to see how the early Christians parented each other so we can begin to do the same today.

Day 1 >

Acts 16:1-5

Thus begins one of the greatest partnerships in history. Timothy became Paul's right-hand man and carried the torch after Paul was martyred. Paul wasn't just interested in telling people about Jesus; he was also interested in reproducing Himself as a minister. Timothy's dad most likely wasn't a believer so Paul took him in and trained him like a son. Because of this long-term personal treatment, Timothy became a trusted friend and minister in his own right. God is calling us to spread the gospel but also to train those less spiritually-mature to walk with Christ. No matter where you are in your journey, you can always help those younger in the faith than yourself.

Who are some of your spiritual mentors?

Who are the younger believers you help—or could help—in their walk with Christ?

Day 2 >>

Mark 5:37; Mark 9:2; Mark 14:33-34

While Jesus spent His ministry preaching and teaching all over Israel, He also poured a lot of time into His twelve disciples. Even among them He had three that He spent extra time with. Jesus knew it would take more than mass preaching to

community: The New Testament Church—The Essence of Fellowship

bring about the Kingdom of God; it would take lifelong relationships. Ultimately, Jesus' grand plan for discipleship was not to tell the entire world about His Father, but to invest His life in a few souls who would invest in others who would do likewise until the task was accomplished.

Is someone pouring his or her life into you right now—like Jesus did with the disciples?

If not, pray that God would send that person into your life.

Ask the Father to show you who you can begin pouring into as well.

Day 3 >>>
Titus 2:3-5

Whose job is it to be a spiritual parent? It's easy to think that teaching others how to be godly is a pastor's job—or at least someone with more experience than you. Almost everyone thinks that way. If you wait until you think you're ready to teach others, you'll never actually teach anyone. Here Paul exhorted Titus to encourage the women in the church to train the ladies who are younger than them. It's not just the job for a few but for every person in the church. The same could be said for the men of the church. Mentoring younger believers is everyone's job, including yours. Don't worry; Jesus is not asking you to be a spiritual parent to everyone, but keep your eyes open for the few people you could have a special impact on.

How can you begin mentoring younger believers in your church?

Is there anything in your life that would hinder you from taking on such a role? If so, what is it? Ask God to help you deal with it immediately.

Day 4 >>>>
Philippians 1:3-11

Paul was no fly-by-night con artist. When he came to plant a church he would often spend months or even years helping it get on its feet before he moved on. Because of this, those churches were very dear to his heart. They were literally like children to him. Many of the letters we read today in the New Testament are letters Paul wrote to the churches he had started. Even though he couldn't be with them physically, he wanted them to know he loved them, prayed for them, and was thinking about them. Your encouragement can go a long way in the lives of those you love.

Who do you encourage on a regular basis?

Ask God to remind you of some people you could encourage today with a word, a phone call, or an email. Then do it!

Day 5 >>>>>
2 Corinthians 6:3-13

Being a parent isn't easy. (Go ask your mom or dad if you don't believe me!) Sometimes even the people we are trying to help the most won't appreciate what we are trying to do for them. The Corinthians here casually disregarded Paul even after all he had done for them. This hurt Paul just like it would hurt us if our efforts were ignored. But Paul didn't give up on them. (The letter of 2 Corinthians is proof enough of that.) When those we are trying to train don't respond as we'd like, remember that helping people grow is a long-term process. It's not about a one-month or two-month commitment but a lifetime of sharing your life with them. Look past your own hurt and see the big picture. The people we are trying to help will probably eventually come around, but we have to stay committed.

Have you ever been ignored after investing a lot in someone?

How did you handle it?

Ask God to help you persevere in helping others—even when they don't give much back in return.

Going to Macedonia
Paul's Vision

memory verse

During the night Paul had a vision of a man of Macedonia standing and begging him, "Come over to Macedonia and help us." After Paul had seen the vision, we got ready at once to leave for Macedonia, concluding that God had called us to preach the gospel to them. **Acts 16:9-10**

Wouldn't it be great if we had road signs for life? Signs like, "College, Turn Here," or, "Character Work Next Four Months." It might not make life easier, but we would be a little more confident about which choices to make. These signs would be helpful in our spiritual lives as well. But unfortunately there are no such signs.

Some people think following God is easy; usually it is anything but easy. One of the frustrating aspects of following God is that we often don't know where we're going. We may have one idea about how to serve God only to discover He wants us to do something else. This can be frustrating and even defeating if we're not careful.

Don't think you are alone in this. Even the apostles had experiences like ours. Acts 16 records a story of how Paul went through some frustration before finally finding God's will concerning the next phase of his ministry. This week we're going to look at how Paul dealt with this change of plans and see what resulted.

So often we can only see the next step in our journey. Our limited perspective means we don't always know what's best for us. God can see our entire journey. When He asks us to make sacrifices or change our plans, it is always in our best interest to obey. The result honors God and brings us to the best possible place in our own lives. So put on your traveling shoes; we're about to make a detour.

Day 1 >
Acts 16:6-10

Paul just wanted to preach. He was so passionate to see people saved that he would have gone anywhere to share Jesus with them. But on occasion God had very specific plans for Paul and company. By pointing them to Macedonia (present-day Greece) the gospel penetrated Europe for the first time. Europe later became the center of Christianity for centuries.

Of course, Paul had no knowledge of this and simply went where the Spirit led. We will not always get such specific guidance, but when we do we should always heed it even if we don't see the reason why. You probably knew that. But why is it that we so rarely listen for God's direction?

Do you take time to regularly listen for the voice of God?

If God asked you to do something you didn't completely understand, would you trust Him anyway? Why or why not?

Day 2 >>
Acts 16:11-15

Put yourself in Paul's shoes. All he wanted to do was tell people about Jesus. He even had a personal encounter with Jesus telling him to do just that. But for some reason God wouldn't let him preach in the provence of Asia. He had the right motive and the right mission, so what was the problem? Sometimes God's will just doesn't make sense to us. Sometimes He will ask us to forego something we really want, even when it's a godly request. This doesn't mean He's angry or that what you requested was wrong. It just means He has a better plan in mind. We have to learn to trust Him even when it doesn't make sense to us.

Has God ever denied a request you thought was godly?

How did you respond?

Ask God to give you the faith to obey even when all the reasons aren't apparent.

Day 3 >>>
Jeremiah 20:7-9

Jeremiah was called to be a prophet as a young boy. But fulfilling that calling was easier said than done. Jeremiah lamented so much about the things he had to preach that he is now called "the weeping prophet." Why was it so hard for Jeremiah to do his job? Because no one listened. We live in a sinful world where God is not honored universally. When we do our best to obey Him we will almost always face opposition. But opposition doesn't mean you're off track. Struggle typically means

you are right where you need to be. Following God's will isn't always this hard, but it's not always easy either. Don't judge your place in God's will by your circumstances or how you feel. Instead, trust in the Lord who called you in the first place.

What has been the hardest thing you had to do to obey God?

Ask God today for a determination like Jeremiah—to obey even when it is hard.

Day 4 >>>>
Philippians 4:14-19

Remember that Paul didn't originally want to go to Europe. But there he was anyway because that's where God wanted him. He probably went kind of reluctantly, especially if he had his heart set on the provence of Asia. But look at the results. One of the first places Paul planted a church in was Philippi, which turns into not only an amazingly healthy church, but one of Paul's favorites. In today's passage we find out they supported him when no other church would. You may find yourself having to give up something you love or enjoy for an uncertain future. Just like moving to a new town, it's hard to give up the good you have for the good you don't know about. But trust in God is always rewarded. Change is hard, but when God calls us to change, it will always lead to something better.

What do you think would have happened if Paul hadn't obeyed God and had gone to the provence of Asia instead?

Will you obey even if it means giving up something you love or enjoy?

Day 5 >>>>>
Numbers 13:1-10

I would not have wanted Moses' job! Any time there was a problem, the whole nation talked about going back to Egyptian slavery. Even here, on the verge of the Promised Land, the people didn't want to go in because they were going to have to fight for it. These people would have settled for living in slavery or in the desert instead of trusting God and moving forward. As silly as this seems, we do this all the time when we are not willing to follow God forward in faith. Faith by its very nature is difficult, but when we choose to follow God instead of the status quo we will find ourselves in the land flowing with milk and honey—and not out in the cold.

Are there any places in your life where you don't want to follow God in faith?

What are they?

Are you complacently settling for the present instead of trusting God with the future?

Singing in the Jail
Paul and Silas in Prison

memory verse

He then brought them out and asked, "Sirs,
what must I do to be saved?" They replied,
"Believe in the Lord Jesus, and you will
be saved—you and your household."
Acts 16:30-31

H ave you ever hit your funny bone?
You know what I'm talking about,
although I'm sure this is not the technical name for it. Often I have hit my
elbow and felt a shooting pain, but right
after also a desire to laugh. My arm
hurts, but it makes me laugh, too. It's
weird how pain and laughter can coexist.
It doesn't make sense, but it happens.

This week we're looking at an equally
improbable event. Paul and Silas were
beaten and thrown in prison, but then led
a worship service in their jail cell. How can
someone experience such pain yet still
find it in them to sing? Our reaction to
bad situations is one way we show a lost
world that Christ is real. When we are able
to see Christ in the midst of our pain,
we find strength where others find only
emptiness and despair.

Like Shadrach, Meshach, and Abednego,
if we turn our troubles over to God, we
discover that He walks with us in the fire.
And when we get out, everyone marvels
at the fact that God actually provided help
in the times of pain. God can help us
become people who react like Paul and
Silas. The bad news is it usually takes a
lot of tough experiences to build that
kind of character. But we have to start
somewhere. And we don't have to do
it alone.

Day 1 >

Acts 16:16-34

They did what? How in the world do you find time to sing your favorite worship chorus when your back is on fire from your latest beating, and you can't get to sleep because of the pain? Yet here they are, responding as Christ would. And that's really the key here. If you're saying to yourself, "I couldn't do that," you may be right. But how can you get to where you could? Not by trying really hard to sing when you hurt. These guys sang because that was what came out of them; it was their character. When we are really hard pressed during difficult times, what is deep in us will come out. Don't try to make it happen; ask God to change you to the point that this will be your natural reaction.

How do you think you would have responded in this situation?

Ask God to change who you are deep down, not just on the surface.

Day 2 >>

2 Corinthians 1:3-7

Never forget verse three: our God is the God of all comfort. No matter how you feel, this is God's nature; He longs to help us and comfort us when we are hurting.

community: The New Testament Church—The Essence of Fellowship

Sometimes that help doesn't come in the way we want, but that doesn't change God's nature. When you go to Him for help, He will provide. Period. But note that God wants to comfort us so we can in turn comfort others. When we have been through a rough time and find peace in the midst of strife, we are able to go to others who are still in the fight and show them that they can survive with God's help just like we did. When we do this it causes us to begin loving those who hurt. As we comfort others, we are becoming more like Christ.

How has God been the God of all comfort to you?

How can you help those who are going through struggles similar to yours?

Day 3 >>>
2 Corinthians 1:8-11

If Paul had times in his life that made him think he was going to die, I'm sure we will have our share of difficult days as well. Think about it: Paul was very close to God but still had moments where he wondered what was going on. When you face harsh circumstances, it's normal to be afraid, to wonder where God is, and to hate the pain . . . but you still get to choose how to respond. Paul saw the bigger picture; he didn't need to rely on his own power—but on God's—to get through trials. It's easy to try to manage on our own, but God asks us to have faith in Him, even in—especially in—the midst of our pain.

Think through your latest trial and note how you responded.

Did you rely on God's power or your own?

Ask God to show you how to respond like Paul in the midst of pain.

Day 4 >>>>

James 1:2-4

This is one of those verses most of us just don't get. In fact, it almost sounds dumb. Why would anyone rejoice over hard times? James was not some sadistic person who thought we should enjoy pain. Instead, He reminded us to look beyond our circumstances to the fact that God is always using our problems for our good. In fact, this becomes a huge encouragement when you are hurting. Problems are hard, but knowing that our struggle isn't in vain helps us endure them a little easier. Nothing that happens to you is wasted by God. Even if Satan means it for evil, God turns it around for good. Knowing this doesn't stop the pain, but it can help us find joy in the pain.

How has God used past hurts to help you now?

Thank God for being present in the midst of our trials and for using them in ways we can't see . . . yet.

Day 5 >>>>>
Acts 16:25-30

Just as God never fails to use our trials for our good, He also uses our responses to turn a bad situation into a good one. The effect of Paul and Silas's response to their torture was so stunning that even when the prison doors flew open, the other prisoners refused to leave. Imagine that! They would rather stay in the jail with the people who could find joy in a prison than leave and go back to lives beyond their cell. The jailer was so moved he became a Christian moments later. Our trials are not just about us! When we see that God was using this trial to help others, it can give us the confidence to continue trusting God even though the pain is still real.

Ask the Father to show you how He has used your reactions to help others.

Try to look beyond your own pain today and see how God can use you in the midst of it.

The Unknown God
Paul in Athens

memory verse

For he has set a day when he will judge the world with justice by the man he has appointed. He has given proof of this to all men by raising him from the dead."

Acts 17:31

Imagine you got a chance to travel back in time and explore your favorite period of history. It sounds great at first, but then try explaining to people in that time about the world you live in. How would you describe electricity to someone from the Middle Ages? Those people would have a hard time understanding you because they have no frame of reference. Since they've never even imagined some of the things you're talking about, they'd probably give you some funny looks. In Acts 17:16-34, Paul found himself in a similar situation as he tried to explain Christ to people in Athens who had no frame of reference for a resurrected Messiah. While some people thought Paul was crazy, Paul got through to the Athenians by finding out what they knew and starting from there.

Witnessing to people isn't easy, but if we love them we'll do our best to paint a clear picture for them. There are more people around you than you know who have no idea what a personal relationship with Jesus is—or how to have one. And you may be the only person they know who can tell them. What will you say? Like Paul, this week we're going to figure out a game plan so we can meet people where they are and take the gospel to those who may have never heard His name.

community: The New Testament Church—The Essence of Fellowship

Day 1 >
Acts 17:16-34

How do you talk to people who don't even have a basic, foundational starting point for the God you want to talk about? One idea is to find something they do know about and start from there. Witnessing isn't just about spouting recited lines to lost people. You can't just ask people if they want to be "washed in the blood of the lamb" if they don't know what you're talking about. They might think you're some psychotic sheep rancher. Loving people means understanding them first and then explaining the love of Jesus in a way they can grasp. We must start where they are, not where we are. In today's verses Paul did that. He found some who were very receptive. Before you start witnessing to people, find out about them. Who are they? What are they like? It can make all the difference.

How would you begin to share Christ with someone who has never been to church?

Write out your testimony without using any church language at all.

Day 2 >>
1 Corinthians 9:19-23

You never can quite put Paul in a box. As soon as you think you have him figured out, he'll surprise you. Why? Paul didn't think of himself all that much. Instead, he thought about the people who needed Christ and how best to reach them. He knew that one approach wouldn't reach everyone, so he decided to keep changing his approach to reach as many as possible. Reaching out means that we start with others, not ourselves. It means you ask the question, "How can I explain Christ in a way that they can hear and understand?" The answer will most likely be different for almost everyone you meet. But you will also find yourself with more of an audience for your message.

Are you willing to go into someone else's world to share the gospel with them— or do you ask them to come to yours?

What would you look like if you became "all things to all people"?

Day 3 >>>
Acts 17:24-28; Ecclesiastes 3:11

"But they're not going to listen to me!" How many times has this excuse kept you from sharing Christ with others? In this passage, Paul was talking to people who were the complete opposite of the God-fearing Jews in the synagogue. Paul was confident they would listen because although they're different, they were also human. God has put a longing in every person to seek Him. Everyone knows deep down that we're made to be more than mere mortals. So even though everyone looks and sounds different, God knows what's going on in their hearts. No matter who you are talking to, you can always bank on this. They may not look like it; they may never tell you; they may not even understand it themselves; but everyone you know has a longing for God.

How does this knowledge change how you interpret the reactions of those you share Christ with?

Spend some time thinking about how your lost friends are actually seeking eternal things—whether they know it or not.

Day 4 >>>>
1 Peter 2:11-12

St. Francis once said, "Preach the gospel; use words if necessary." When we reach out to those who don't know God, the first thing they evaluate is our behavior. In fact, some may not listen to our words until our behavior proves that we are different. Not everyone understands theology, but everyone sees that you are different when you love at times when others would hate, give at times when others would take, and pray at times when others would curse. Practical acts of love and service are surefire ways of opening doors to tell others why you live the way you live. Does it take longer? Sure, but it works. Does your lifestyle help or hurt your ability to share the gospel with others?

How can you live today in a way that preaches the gospel without words?

Day 5 >>>>>
1 Corinthians 2:1-5

Have you ever started witnessing to someone only to find yourself in a religious debate? It's frustrating and usually unproductive. We can usually avoid this if we stay focused. If not we'll end up talking to people about the problems and consequences of sin without ever getting to the core issue: their need for Christ. Talking to a homosexual about his lifestyle without addressing his need for Christ addresses a symptom of sin (homosexuality) but won't cure the illness (sin nature).

Don't get sidetracked by secondary issues; instead, make sure the focus is on Jesus. His death on the cross is the answer for all of us. Let Him deal with all the issues in His time. We need to stay focused on His life, death, and resurrection.

When you talk to others about Jesus, do you talk more about His rules or His salvation?

Ask Jesus to help you focus on Him alone today as you tell others about Him.

A Night's Vision
Paul in Corinth

memory verse

One night the Lord spoke to Paul in a vision: "Do not be afraid; keep on speaking, do not be silent. For I am with you, and no one is going to attack and harm you, because I have many people in this city." **Acts 18:9-10**

While on a mission trip to Mexico some cops rounded up a bunch of guys in our worship service and led them out past me. One told me these were some local gang members causing trouble. I asked if they could stay, but I was ignored. "Too bad," I thought. "I wish they could have heard the gospel." Suddenly I felt God leading me to tell these guys about Jesus. My response to God was that talking to gang members was not my spiritual gift. God didn't buy it. So, scared to death, I went off into the parking lot chasing twelve gang members to tell them about Christ.

My situation was a cake walk compared to what Paul endured. As he traveled on his missionary journeys, people routinely wanted to kill him. This always makes me wonder if Paul ever got scared like I did? The anwer must be yes, since in Acts 18 God gave Paul a special vision reminding Paul that He would always be with him. Armed with that confidence, Paul never wavered as he preached and taught.

God may ask us to do things that are frightening, but He will always be with us. Our fear may not go away completely, but we can have faith in God that He will not let us down. This week we'll look at how to find courage in the midst of difficult ministry moments.

Day 1 >

Acts 18:9-17

Paul wasn't paranoid; people really were trying to kill him! It's one thing to tell others about Jesus. It's quite another to tell people about Him when they may want to kill you afterwards. Paul was reassured by God that he would be protected. God kept His promise. When the Jews tried to get Paul beaten by the Romans, the Romans did not find him guilty. In fact, the only one beaten that day was one of Paul's accusers. God promises in Scripture to help us stand firm in the face of opposition. This passage proves that, as we obey God, He will do what He said He would do.

Where are some places in your life where you are tempted to back down from doing what you know you need to do?

Which promises of God do you rely on to avoid those temptations? Write them here—or find some today.

Day 2 >>

Jeremiah 9:23-24

Strength and confidence come from many places. Some people are confident because they are popular, wealthy, or talented. The problem is that none of these things are stable enough to be relied upon.

We need to always be on guard against false pride. We may feel we're walking tall with the Lord, but where does that confidence come from? Is it because we really know Him or because we simply look good to others? In order to walk in courage and humility, we must always be developing a real relationship with God, not just going through the motions. Any other type of confidence will ultimately fail us. Remember: There is nothing more important than your personal walk with the Lord!

Where does your confidence come from?

How can you gain real confidence?

What do you learn about God from this passage?

Spend some time talking to God about these attributes.

Day 3 >>>
Joshua 1:1-9

Imagine you've just been handed the leadership over a million people. You're about to go start a war with ten other nations, and you have no idea what you're doing. No pressure, right? No wonder God gave this advice to young Joshua: Don't fear!

Having faith and moving forward is always accompanied with at least some fear, since we're being asked to do something we couldn't do on our own. But we can never let fear keep us from being faithful. This is courage: when we choose to obey even when we're uncertain. Following Christ demands courage even if you have a little less responsibility than Joshua. No one said this would be easy. But God promised He will be with us every step of the way.

God gives Joshua two commands and a promise in this passage. What are they?

How are you obeying these same commands that were given to Joshua?

Day 4 >>>>
Acts 18:11; 19:10; 20:31

Paul was no fly-by-night preacher. He knew that in order to have an effective ministry he couldn't just preach a sermon someplace and expect that to fix all the problems. So he ended up staying in certain towns for months and even years. But the fruits of his labors were churches that lasted for decades and centuries.

Sometimes the hard part of ministry is sticking with it. The temptation to quit may not come from a physical threat, but from the day-to-day exhaustion of keeping up. The courageous thing is to keep going. Courage sometimes means refusing to quit and seeing God's will through to the end.

community: The New Testament Church—The Essence of Fellowship

Have you ever just wanted to quit being faithful?

How can the results of Paul's ministry in Acts encourage you to persevere?

Ask God for the strength to continue when you have no strength left.

Day 5 >>>>>
2 Timothy 2:1

At one time, this was a confusing verse to me. How can grace make you strong? If I need grace, doesn't it mean that I need help? How can that make me strong?

Paul wasn't protected because he worked hard or was more holy than others. He was protected because God loved Him. We don't need to be strong in our own abilities, but rather strong in God's amazing and unfailing love for us. No matter who you are or what you have done, if you are a believer you can be strong in God's grace instead of trying to do things on your own—and I guarantee it's easier to live in the grace of God than trying to live life solo.

What would it look like for you to be strong in the grace of Jesus Christ?

Ask God for help to live in His grace and not in our own abilities.

The Church Expectant
The Return of Christ

memory verse

For to me, to live is Christ
and to die is gain.
Philippians 1:21

As a kid, I never could sleep on Christmas Eve. I was too excited. Who knew what would be waiting for me under the tree when I got up? Would I get all the things I asked for? Expectation is a powerful force in our lives. It gives us hope, makes us excited, and helps us overcome obstacles and setbacks. But as believers, we aren't waiting for a present under a tree; we are waiting for the return of Christ!

As Paul traveled on his missionary journeys, he wrote to churches he had visited or helped start. These letters would become many of the books of the New Testament. While on his second missionary journey, Paul wrote to the church in Thessalonica. Like a child on Christmas morning, the members of the church were anxious for the return of Christ. But they also had some questions, among them, "What happens to those people who died before Christ came to earth?" Paul answered their questions in 1 Thessalonians 4:13-18.

When Jesus comes again everything will change. We'll get new bodies, we'll see our loved ones who have died, and we'll live forever with God. In the meantime, God has given us a task to accomplish, and it may not always be easy. But if we keep our eyes focused on heaven, we'll remember what we're fighting for. We should never settle for sin.

This week we'll look at the future of the church and how that future helps us live here and now.

Day 1 >

1 Thessalonians 4:13-18

A lot of people—Christians and non-Christians—wonder what life will be like in heaven. For example, will we remember our loved ones and will they remember us? Paul told us in today's Scripture passage that when Jesus returns we'll all meet Him in the air together. And though our bodies will be changed, our souls will not. So when we meet Him, we will still be who we are and our loved ones will be as well. They will certainly remember us and vice versa. It's a reunion you don't want to miss!

Pray today for your lost friends to be saved.

Look for opportunities to share Christ with them so they will join you on the day of the Lord's return.

Day 2 >>

Revelation 21:1-5; 21:22-22:5

We have a lot to look forward to! It's always great when God blesses us here, but we need to remember that this is not our home. Don't get too comfortable here, because ultimately we're moving for good. God is preparing something better for us and that's where we will spend eternity. Eternity! In that place there will be no mourning or pain, so when we face pain in this life we need to always remember the future that is to come. It may be hard to be motivated by a place we've never seen, but as we dwell on our eternal destiny it gives us the courage to face the pain we sometimes experience here.

Have you ever seriously thought about heaven before?

Spend some time trying to picture what heaven is like.

Thank God for preparing such an awesome place for us.

Day 3 >>>
1 Corinthians 15:50-56

The number one fear is the fear of death. And rightly so; it destroys all of what we have created for ourselves. Some people will do anything to get away from death. But for those of us who know we will live forever with Christ, there's no need to worry. While thinking about death may make us a little uncomfortable, Christ has taken its ultimate effects away for Christians. So we can face death with dignity and expectation and without fear. As Paul would later say, "I can either stay here and serve Christ or go to be with Him, either one is fine with me."

Are you afraid of death?

community: The New Testament Church—The Essence of Fellowship

Spend some time with this passage and apply it to yourself.

Ask God to help you live without that fear today.

Day 4 >>>>
Acts 20:17-38

If we know that we'll be reunited with our loved ones after death, is it natural to mourn when they die? Of course it is. Even Jesus wept at the death of Lazarus, though He knew He would raise him moments later. In today's passage, Paul's friends wept over him because they know they won't see him again before the resurrection. If we have real love for one another, it is perfectly natural to mourn someone's passing. However, we don't mourn as the world mourns because we know that this is just a brief separation; it's not permanent. We still cry, though, because we love them. Mourning is a healthy part of dealing with death so we can move on with our lives.

Have you ever lost a loved one or a close friend?

Give yourself the freedom to mourn their loss, but always remember that if they are Christians, you will see them again.

Day 5 >>>>>

2 Corinthians 5:6-8

Knowing that we are heading home to be with the Lord helps us understand this statement: "We live by faith, not by sight." Faith in what? Faith that everything the Lord told us is real. We really will be raised from the dead! We really will live with Him forever!

When we know that we have a future in heaven and that we will be held account-able for all our actions, we will make better decisions here on earth. Unfortunately, many live under a different philosophy: "Out of sight, out of mind." How you live is determined by which philosophy you choose. Remembering our heavenly home helps us stay on track and live as an expectant body of believers.

Which statement best describes how you actually live—"The present affects the future" or "Out of sight, out of mind"?

Ask the Father to give you a clear picture of your future and to help you live by faith—not by sight.

community: The New Testament Church—The Essence of Fellowship

Spiritual Opposition
The Riot at Ephesus and the 3rd Missionary Journey

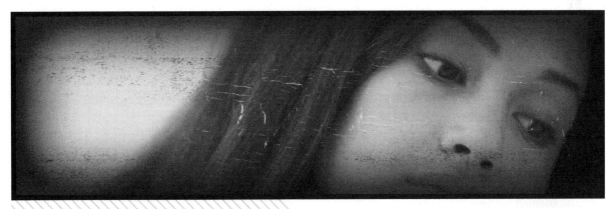

Be self-controlled and alert. Your enemy the devil prowls around like a roaring lion looking for someone to devour. **1 Peter 5:8**

Whenever I think of demons, those stone gargoyles found on old buildings come to mind. Big fangs and ugly face but definitely stone. It's kind of hard to think of something like that being a real threat in my life. Isn't a belief in demons about as outdated as the buildings those gargoyles sit on? Surprisingly, no. Demons are real, and they take every chance to stand in your way spiritually.

In Acts 19:21-41, Paul and his fellow travelers faced some pretty significant opposition. But look closer. The real reason behind the opposition was spiritual; these people were worshipers of a false god. They wanted nothing more than to be rid of Paul and his companions . . . by any means necessary.

You may not have to deal with physical opposition, but you will definitely have to deal with spiritual warfare. You're in for it whether you like it or not. But how do you fight an invisible enemy, and what do spiritual battles feel like? This week we're going to take a look at the invisible war we are fighting as Christians and hopefully find answers to some of your questions. Try to see beyond the visible this week and recognize what's really happening in the spiritual realm.

Day 1 >

Acts 19:21-41; Ephesians 6:12

This was another close shave for Paul, but look at how he interpreted it. When he wrote to the Ephesians later he didn't warn them against the same men who tried to kill him, even though they were still around. Instead, he warned them about the spiritual forces that were behind the attack in the first place. Paul knew where the real threat lay: in the spiritual forces of darkness. Now don't go weird on me; it's not necessary to worry about demons leaping out from every corner you see. (My car won't start—it must be a demon!) But our spiritual enemies are very real. Do you think they decided to quit after Jesus ascended to heaven? If they harassed Him, they will harass us too.

How does knowing you will face spiritual opposition change your outlook toward being a Christian?

Day 2 >>

Ephesians 6:13-19

This is one of those passages that everyone knows . . . but what do you do with it? Is there some sort of spiritual kung fu we can learn? Well, no, but that's not really necessary. Look at the things that make up the armor. Each of them are things we use on a daily basis (or at least should use): faith,

righteousness, truth. Fighting spiritual battles has less to do with praying unusual spiritual prayers ("Demon, come out!") and much more to do with living an authentic Christian life day in and day out. Using your faith, being prepared to share the gospel, and knowing God's Word are real weapons that will result in real results in the spiritual battles you face.

What are some spiritual battles you feel you are fighting right now?

How can you use your spiritual armor to fight those battles? Be specific . . . and then go try these strategies out.

Day 3 >>>
2 Corinthians 10:3-7

The Corinthians thought that Paul was all bark and no bite since he apparently wasn't all that intimidating to look at. Paul reminds them, however, that all is not always as it seems. He may not have looked powerful, but his power came from his God—and his weapons were more powerful than you can imagine.

Never underestimate the war we are in, but also don't underestimate the power you have in Christ to fight it. Paul told us to take every thought captive and to make them obedient to Christ. So as you go through your day be aware of the spiritual

things that are going on. Don't be afraid
to jump in and stand up for God's truth.

Read today's Scripture passage again.
How can you accomplish these tasks
in your daily life?

Ask God to show you places where you
can take thoughts captive for Him today.

Day 4 >>>>
1 Peter 5:8-9

Have you ever noticed that we deal with
a lot more temptation when we're alone
than when we're with other people? One
of the main tactics Satan will use is to
attack us when we're the weakest, which
is typically when we're alone. I once had
a teacher tell me we'll have a harder time
overcoming temptation when we're
hungry, angry, lonely, or tired—and she
was right! Therefore, Peter tells us to be
alert; he knows Satan is looking for
someone to devour (not some group). Since
Satan is always looking for a weak moment,
we need to be aware of times when we are
most vulnerable. Don't let him surprise
you! Instead, make sure you've always
got good Christian friends you can hang
out with or call when you feel tempted.
Everyone needs that kind of help.

What do you struggle with most when
you're alone?

Have you ever told anyone about it?
Why or why not?

Ask God to help you see temptations
before they become unmanageable.

Day 5 >>>>>

Philippians 4:8-9

Most of the battles for the heart start in the mind. For example, before you actually commit a sin, a battle is fought in your mind over whether you'll commit the sin or not. And it's here the spiritual warfare gets thick. A lot of what goes into our minds, or what we choose to dwell on, actually pushes us toward sin instead of pulling us away from it. So being aware of what is going on in our mind is crucial if we want to win the battle against sin. Why? It's always easier to win a battle in your mind as opposed to trying to get out of a tough situation. If you overcome bad thoughts before they turn into bad actions, you'll find yourself winning every after time. Maybe it's time you shifted the battlefield to your mind.

Does your thought life sound like the verses you read today?

Spend some time today choosing to reject thoughts that lead you away from the qualities in these verses . . . then watch to see if temptations are easier to handle.

Internal Divisions
Paul's Letter to the Corinthians, Part 1

memory verse

Live in harmony with one another. Do not be proud, but be willing to associate with people of low position. Do not be conceited.
Romans 12:16

Have you ever felt betrayed . . . like when you found out your best friend was talking behind your back. It's worse—much worse—than finding out your worst enemy was trashing you. We expect it from our enemies but not our friends! I think we're ready as believers to fight spiritual forces set against us and even other people who don't believe in Christ. But it's a shock to realize you'll often end up fighting against people in your church.

Paul experienced this firsthand. While in Ephesus, on his third missionary journey, Paul wrote to the church in Corinth. After wading through angry mobs of pagans in town after town, he found out that the believers in Corinth were fighting amongst themselves. The same thing happens today. In Ireland, Protestants and Catholics are in a centuries old battle. Almost all of us know of a church that split over some trivial matter like the color of the carpet. What's going on? Satan will never fight fair. If he can sabotage churches, he's more than willing.

This week we'll look at some internal problems that cropped up in the New Testament church and see how God wants us to deal with it. Any conflict can be defeated when we allow Christ and His truth—and not our prideful opinions—to be our guide.

Day 1 >
1 Corinthians 3:1-9

Most of us like to believe we are more mature than we actually are. Like the time you told your parents you were so ready to drive . . . at age thirteen! At times like that we need a reality check, which is exactly what Paul gave the Corinthians here. For all their lofty opinions of themselves, Paul told them he couldn't teach them the really deep parts of the faith because they wouldn't get it. In effect, he said, "Telling you deep things is like trying to explain physics to an eight-year old; you just aren't mature enough to understand it." The Corinthians were capable of maturing so they could hear those things; they just thought they were already mature when they weren't. That kind of pride is costly.

Take an honest inventory of your spiritual life. Are you an infant or are you growing steadily?

Ask the Lord to help you grow day by day so you won't miss out on anything He wants to teach you.

Day 2 >>
2 Corinthians 11

Whoa! How's that for a tirade? If you've never read sarcasm in the Bible, here it is. It seems odd for us, but Paul was actually defending his status as an apostle. Other "super teachers" were trying to put Paul down, saying he wasn't flashy enough and he didn't act like the other charlatans that were running around. Translation for today: he wasn't cool/funny/popular enough. But Paul made no apologies for this. He was more interested in telling people the truth than tickling their ears. We have to be very careful to whom we listen; otherwise, we'll end up like the Corinthians who started dismissing Paul—Paul!—for some other guy who made them laugh. We've always got to be on guard against flashy hypocrites, no matter how cool they seem.

Who do you follow as a spiritual leader? Why?

Ask the Lord to show you who true spiritual leaders are and how to spot imposters before they lead you astray.

Day 3 >>>
Philippians 4:2-3

I know this never happens in your church, but apparently in the Philippian church some women weren't getting along. Disagreements are a common—yet costly—problem. When people hold grudges, get angry, or refuse to compromise, they end up spending precious time and energy putting out relational fires instead of focusing on the work God has for them. Satan can't

community: The New Testament Church—The Essence of Fellowship

destroy the church, but He can get us side-tracked. Prompting fights between church members is an easy way to accomplish that.

If you find yourself in a disagreement with someone at church, make every effort possible to resolve the situation quickly by practicing patience and forgiveness. I know: That's easier said than done, but it's more important than you know. And we can't afford to put off the work of God.

Are you in a situation right now like these two women?

Why can't it be resolved today?

Spend some time today praying for wisdom, patience, and a spirit of forgiveness.

Day 4 >>>>
1 Corinthians 1:8

The Corinthian church had a lot of issues that Paul tried to tackle. That's probably why 1 Corinthians is such a long letter. One of the main issues was that the Corinthians thought they knew it all. The problem was that their pride led them to hurt each other. They started to focus on minor things (like being able to eat whatever they wanted) instead of major things (like loving their fellow church members). Paul told them to get off their pedestals and see what was happening. I don't think anyone does it on purpose, but we can drift in a prideful direction if we're not careful.

Are there any ways you think you are more spiritual than most?

Ask God to reveal any places where your pride is causing you or others to stumble.

Day 5 >>>>>
Romans 12:17

It's a sad reality that people hurt us occasionally—intentionally or unintentionally. We don't have any control over that, but we do have control over our response. Paul reminded us to react as Jesus did, and he even gave us a reason why: God will ultimately deal with all wrongs. So we don't have to get revenge; God will deal justly with everyone. God's answer when we get hurt is not, "Get over it;" it's "I'll take care of it; just trust Me." Knowing that, it's easier to allow God to resolve situations instead of addressing them ourselves.

Is there any situation in which you refuse to live at peace with someone?

According to this Scripture, what should you do?

Ask the Father to help you give Him control of the difficult situations of your life.

week 30 <<<
Accountability
Paul's Letter to the Corinthians, Part 2

memory verse

Brothers, if someone is caught in a sin, you who are spiritual should restore him gently. But watch yourself, or you also may be tempted.
Galatians 6:1

I never would have survived high school without my best friends. Together we had some of the best years of our lives, but we also kept each other from straying away from Christ. We were accountable to one another. In week nine we figured out that if we're going to have integrity as a church, we can't let sin go unchecked. That's easy enough when we're the problem, but it gets a little harder when we have to tell someone else that what they're doing is wrong. That's where accountability comes in.

As Paul planted churches, he didn't forget about them once he left. While he traveled, he routinely kept track of them and even made return visits to make sure they stayed healthy. Paul found out the Corintians were allowing sin to go unchecked, so he wrote to keep them accountable to their commitment to Christ.

Every now and then we'll have friends who stray off the path. When that happens we need to be there to help them get back on the right track, just like we'll need them to help us. I know it sounds unpleasant, and it can get messy. But when we actually start holding each other accountable, you will be surprised how much it helps your own spiritual life. Instead of dealing with sin on your own, you can tackle it with the help of your Christian friends. But it starts when we are honest about our own lives and are open to listening to others when they confront us.

Ready? Let's figure out this week how we can hold each other accountable.

Day 1 >

1 Corinthians 5:1-13

Sin is serious; apparently the Corinthians had forgotten. Paul was furious. The church failed to see the danger in allowing a sinful activity to go unchecked. Paul demanded they stop allowing such behavior. He told them to exclude the immoral person from the church. This "handing over to Satan" would hopefully help this person see that his actions were incompatible with godly living, prompting him to repent and return. Sound too harsh? Remember, sin is serious. But the goal was not to have him remain outside. Paul's love was tough love, but it was love in it's truest form, a love that wouldn't allow a friend to destroy himself.

Do you know a Christian who is consistently living in an ungodly way?

How would Paul command you deal with this person?

Are you living in a way that is consistently ungodly? What can you do to address your sinful actions?

Day 2 >>

Matthew 18:15-20

It would be great if we all figured everything out on the first try, but it usually doesn't work that way. Sometimes we must confront our friends. Jesus knew this was complicated, so He set guidelines for how to confront fellow believers when they sin. Keeping the situation between the two of you is best. If the situation can be resolved without involving other people, it will prevent gossip and other issues. But if your friend resists listening to you, try a small group. As a last resort the whole church should be informed, and here the church leadership should be involved. These guidelines not only protect the person being confronted, but it keeps us in check as well.

Have you ever had to confront someone about a sin that you noticed in his or her life? How did it go?

Would these guidelines have helped?

Pray for the patience to humbly walk with someone if God calls you to a confrontation.

Day 3 >>>
Psalm 141:3-5

Now here's an odd scene. David was actually praying that his friends would punch him and tell him he was wrong. What's going on here? David had already figured out that at times he preferred to do the wrong thing. (Can you relate?) On some occasions he deliberately committed sin and paid the price. The other thing he knew was that he had friends who would tell him the truth. But no one wants to be told they're wrong. So he made a commitment to listen to his friends when they held him accountable. Your truest friends are those who will love you enough to let you know when you're wrong. You may need them more than you know. If David needed accountability, I'm pretty sure we do, too.

Do you have friends who love you enough to tell you you're wrong?

Do you love your friends enough to help them see when they're sinning and hurting themselves?

Ask God to provide those friends for you and to help you be that kind of friend.

Day 4 >>>>
Matthew 7:1-5

Have you ever met someone who loved to point out your faults but would never acknowledge they had done anything wrong? Accountability is important, but we need to remember that God has not called us to be everyone else's watchdog. The Father calls us to help each other get through sin, but first we need to recognize where we are failing. Checking yourself before you confront someone helps you in two ways. First, it helps you sympathize with someone as a fellow sinner. Next, it

community: The New Testament Church—The Essence of Fellowship

protects you from pridefully thinking you are better than the other person. People are much more willing to listen when they feel understood.

All of us have sinned; does that mean we shouldn't confront others when they sin?

What does the passage say?

Ask God to keep you humble—but firm—as you interact with others.

Day 5 >>>>>
Galatians 6:1-5

When I think about accountability, I think about telling someone they're wrong. But Paul knew that it was much more than that. He describes accountability as helping carry each other's burdens. If we are really helping each other in love, we're not just concerned with telling someone their faults. Instead, we're willing to help them walk out of that bad situation. This is what real love looks like. If we're not willing to help someone walk the hard road out of sin, we may not be ready to confront that person. Real accountability is a long-term process, not a one time reprimand. This is what Christ does for us . . . and what He is calling us to do for others.

Think about some ways you can carry your friends' burdens today.

The Lord's Supper
Paul's Letter to the Corinthians, Part 3

memory verse

God has raised this Jesus to life, and we are all witnesses of the fact. **Acts 2:32**

Little cups filled with grape juice. Little pieces of bland bread. Must be communion again. The Lord's Supper is something we've probably all participated in, but do we actually understand what's going on? In the early Roman world some people feared Christians since one of their rituals supposedly included cannibalism (at least that's what some people thought was going on). They had heard that to be a Christian you had to eat the body and blood of Jesus. I guess to an outsider it sounds strange, but the Lord's Supper is an intimate and precious thing to a Christian.

Jesus left us two major ordinances that we are to participate in as a church; the Lord's Supper is one we are to practice regularly. It's a continual reminder of Christ's sacrifice and constant union with us. If we don't keep this in mind we could miss out on the spiritual impact the Lord's Supper can bring. Paul taught the churches to practice the Lord's Supper but had harsh words for those like the Corinthians who failed to approach the communion table properly.

Does the Lord's Supper make sense to you? It is one of the most intensely personal traditions in which we participate. This week we're going to spend some time looking into what happens when we take communion. Why did Jesus tell us to keep doing it? What's it about anyway? Look deep this week; there may be much more going on than you've ever imagined.

Day 1 >

1 Corinthians 11:17-29

Yeah, people actually got drunk at the Lord's Supper. Crazy, I know, but true. Jesus started the Lord's Supper with His disciples together, not individually. The Corinthians had missed this and were being selfish during the Lord's Supper, ignoring some of the people they didn't like as much. But the Lord's Supper is not just about your relationship with God, it's about all of us. God means for us to take the Lord's Supper together as a church. When we do so, we are being united to the Lord and to each other. So when you take the Lord's Supper, examine your relationship with God and your relationships with others in the church. If these aren't right, make them right. Otherwise, you are missing the point as the Corinthians did.

Do you ever think about others during the Lord's Supper?

Ask God to show you ways that you can be more united to your church family today.

Day 2 >>

Luke 22:14-20

This story may seem all too familiar to us. Even the setting is familiar: a meal with friends. We probably eat with our friends all the time. No big deal, right? Actually, this was a very special thing. In Jewish culture, to share a meal was an intimate event. To invite someone to a meal was to say, "You are one of the closest people in my life." At His last meal, Jesus didn't have a review of His teachings; He reminded them how they were His friends. So when we take the Lord's Supper, realize that it's not just a ritual. God is literally inviting us into the deepest of friendships. God wants to be united with us, so He invites us to His table.

Do you have a close relationship with God or is it more distant? Why?

Imagine what it was like to be part of the original Lord's Supper.

Day 3 >>>
Luke 18:31-33; 22:19

Let's take some time today to dwell on the body of Christ. When Jesus broke the bread at the Last Supper, He knew that in the next few hours He would be severely beaten and tortured. He knew what was coming and still offered His body to be broken for us. Think about the immensity of that sacrifice. If you knew that you were going to be physically harmed, you would probably avoid the situation. Jesus didn't. Instead He walked into it on purpose, knowing it would cost His very life. He loves you that much! So when we take the bread, we need to remember the magnitude of the sacrifice Jesus made by offering His body to be broken for us.

Spend some time right now just thinking about what it would take to purposefully offer yourself for someone else.

Thank Jesus for His sacrifice for you.

Day 4 >>>>
Luke 22:20; Hebrews 12:4

Today, let's dwell on the blood of Christ. Again, think about what it was like for Jesus at the Last Supper. He passed the cup knowing that in just a few hours He would see His own blood splattered on the ground. He knew that scourging and crucifixion were coming—both excruciatingly painful, bloody affairs.

Read Hebrews 12:4. The author reminded us that our struggles aren't nearly as hard as what Jesus did when He offered His blood for us. His love is that immense; His resolve that firm. So when you look at the cup during the Lord's Supper, realize that Jesus was giving His blood for you—on purpose—so that you could live and have eternal life.

Day 5 >>>>>

1 Corinthians 11:26

The Lord's Supper may seem outdated to you. Maybe you've done it so often that it has lost its meaning. But Jesus meant for the Lord's Supper to be a living reminder for us—not only of what happened but also of what's to come. Jesus died on the cross to show you how much He loved you, but He also did it to make sure you would live with Him forever. This story is not over; He's coming back for us! When we take the Lord's Supper, we need to remember that the Savior who gave us His body and blood will come back to give us a new body as well.

When was the last time you thought about Jesus' return?

Try to live today remembering that Jesus is coming back soon. See what changes in your attitude.

Gifts From God
Spiritual Gifts

memory verse

All these are the work of one and the same Spirit, and he gives them to each one, just as he determines.
I Corinthians 12:11

It may have been a while since you've put a puzzle together, but have you ever really studied a puzzle's pieces? They look like something out of a Picasso painting: multiple legs, odd shaped curves, and no hard edges (except for those blessed corner pieces). None of those pieces seems to be identical. They all have a unique place to fit in the big picture, and the portrait won't be complete until every last one of them is in place.

I don't really understand how to cut puzzle pieces, but I'm sure God does. The Church He is building is made in much the same way. When you become a part of the Church you receive a spiritual gift of some kind. One may be given the ability to lead, another the ability to encourage, and still another the ability to make people feel welcome. No matter who you are, everyone gets a gift. The Church functions like it's supposed to when all of us, like puzzle pieces, fit together and each do our part. Leave a piece out and it's just not the same. Because you have this gift you're a very important—even indispensable—part of the Church. Paul made this a top concern when teaching his churches so they would understand that no one can walk alone. Churches aren't filled with spectators but with unique Christians, each with a role to play in the spiritual masterpiece of the church.

This week we're going to look at what spiritual gifts are and how to determine which gifts you have.

Day 1 >

1 Corinthians 12:4-11

I know it's better to give than to receive, but I still like getting gifts. In fact, I'll take a gift pretty much any day of the week. Why? Well, gifts are for me, right? Well, on birthdays, yes; but in the church, no. God has given you a particular gift on purpose, but not just for your own personal benefit. God gave you a spiritual gift so you could use it to help others in the church as well as yourself. Think about it. Healing, teaching, speaking in tongues —none of these spiritual gifts work properly unless they are directed at others. So if we're going to get the most out of our spiritual gift, we've got to be committed to serve others in the church with it. That's what your gift is for.

How does this thought change how you see your spiritual gift?

How does God want you to use your particular gift to help your church?

Day 2 >>

1 Peter 4:10-11

You may have never thought about your gift, or maybe you've wondered whether you even have one or not. "Sure, pastors have them; but what about me?" Notice in today's Scripture passage that Peter

community: The New Testament Church—The Essence of Fellowship

assumed everyone has a spiritual gift. It's not possible for you not to have one. Peter told them to use their gifts because he knew God had given gifts to each one of them; that's how the church works. If that's true then we should spend some time trying to figure out what our gifts are. Your gift may not jump right out at you, but it also won't be the hardest thing in the world to discover.

Do you know what your spiritual gift is? What is it?

How do you know?

Ask God to help you know what your spiritual gift is.

Day 3 >>>
Romans 12:6-8

Yesterday we figured out that we have a spiritual gift; now, we need to find out what it is. (Notice that Paul—like Peter—assumed that we all have a gift.) In three separate passages Paul listed about twenty gifts, so if you don't see yours on this list, that's OK. (See 1 Cor. 12:8-10, 28.) Depending on your age, it may take some time for your gift to display itself, but that shouldn't stop you from trying to find out what it is. What are the things you love to do most at your church? What are the things that bring you the most joy as a believer? Don't know yet? Then try some things out. Figuring this out may take trial and error, so don't be afraid to jump in and see if something works for you.

Pick a gift you think you might have and try it out this week.

Ask God for discernment to figure out what your gift is.

Day 4 >>>>
1 Corinthians 13

Sometimes we can think our gift is the most important and forget why we have it in the first place. That's what happened in Corinth. The Corinthians spoke in tongues—a lot. This was fine, but they had missed the point of why they were given that gift. Here, Paul reminded them that their great knowledge and their ecstatic speech were useful only if it stemmed from a love for other people. If they didn't have that, then all the speaking in tongues and all the knowledge in the world was useless. Your gift is special, but it's given to help others in love; that is the foundation for all spiritual gifts.

According to today's passage, what's the foundation for all the spiritual gifts?

Ask the Holy Spirit to help you love your church more deeply this week.

Day 5 >>>>>

Romans 12:4-5

Back in the day when I was younger, my family had strings with what seemed like hundreds of Christmas lights on them. The problem was that if you pulled just one light out of the string, the rest of them wouldn't work. If there were 99 perfectly good lights and one was defective, the whole string didn't work. It was very frustrating! But the church is much the same. Whether you like it or not, you need all those other folks in your church. Each of them has a gift that you need to make yours work. If you don't use your gift, everyone else suffers; and your gift won't work right unless it's connected to all the others. There are no loners in God's family, so it's important that we not only use our gifts, but help others discover and use theirs as well. It helps all of us.

How can you help your friends discover their spiritual gifts?

Pray today about how you can use your gift in connection with others at your church.

Giving
Paul's Instructions to the Corinthian Church

memory verse

Each man should give what he has decided in his heart to give, not reluctantly or under compulsion, for God loves a cheerful giver.

2 Corinthians 9:7

Bono, lead singer of the band U2, once said in a song, "The God I believe in isn't short of cash." He was criticizing phony TV preachers for stealing money from unsuspecting people. Lots of people have the same feeling. I meet people all the time who assume the only thing churches are after is your money. But Bono brings up a good point: If God can bless everyone, then why do we have to give—to Him or anyone else for that matter? Can't God just bless people? The answer is that it's actually not about the money.

We have received so much from God, it is only right that we honor Him by giving some of it back. And as we give our resources away it reminds us that the God who gave it to us in the first place will provide what we need. From cover to cover the Bible records how people honored God by giving back to Him. The way we do this is through the local church we are part of.

The early churches exemplified this by giving money to help other churches who were in trouble. Paul not only taught his churches about giving, he gave them an opportunity to give an offering which he personally delivered to the Jerusalem church. The generosity of the early churches is an example that we continue to follow today. This week we're going to look at why we need to give God our time, energy, and money.

Day 1 >
2 Corinthians 9:6-15

It's not always easy to give our money away. We work hard to earn it, and we need it to buy necessities (and maybe some fun things as well). But in this passage, Paul reminded us why it can be easy: God is the great Provider. He owns everything and is always able to provide for you as you provide for others. No matter how much you give, God can always outgive you. Because of this we'll never go without. So it all comes down to a question of trust. Do you really believe that God can provide for you? A very easy way to check is to look and see where your money goes.

Why is it so hard to give sometimes?

Think about some ways God is already providing for you. Ask God for faith to trust Him in the places you are still holding onto your money.

Day 2 >>
Luke 16:10-13

You ought to see a capital M on the word *Money* in today's text. Jesus here reminded us that our money can be very powerful spiritually—so much so that He refers to it as a god. If we aren't careful, it will use us instead of our using it. And it doesn't matter how much you have either. Don't believe me? Try giving some of your money away today and see what feelings immediately come to the surface. You might be surprised how much of a hold it has on you. That's why Jesus tells us that it is important to learn how to use our money well in this life.

How does money affect you? Do you think about it a lot or a little?

Ask God to show you how to keep money in its proper place in your life.

Day 3 >>>
Malachi 3:8-10

Most of us assume that when the paycheck or allowance rolls our way it is ours to do with however we see fit. But here God made a startling claim. Since the Israelites were not giving God the full tithe, He said they were robbing Him! God owns everything and gives generously to each of us. He asks that we acknowledge Him by returning a portion of it, remembering that He will always provide for our needs. To not return a tithe, then, is literally robbing God of what He is due and denying that He gave it to us in the first place. Tithing isn't about your church or your money as much as it is about your relationship with God.

Do you tithe? Why or why not?

How would it change the way you live if you considered everything to be God's first and yours second?

Day 4 >>>>
Malachi 3:8-10

God made a startling statement when he said, "Try Me; just see if I won't come through, and come through *big*!" God is not opposed to wealth or to giving great blessings. When we are committed to Him and give in faith, He is faithful to provide richly for us. In fact, God wants to do this. But remember, the point in all this isn't giving in order to receive blessings, it's living in faith that God is in control and will always provide for us. When we believe this—and live it out— it's easy for God to bless us because He knows we'll use those blessings well.

We ask for a lot from God. How much do you give to Him?

What are some ways you can trust God with your money this week?

Day 5 >>>>>

2 Corinthians 9:6-15

Let's end where we began this week. Why
do we have to give to the church? It's an
honest question. Some people say that
they would rather give to a charity or to
people they know. And that's fine. God
wants us to give where there are needs.
But giving to the church is different. We
know now that we are a part of a body.
So when we give at church, we are taking
care of God's people and God's plan to
reach the world. When you give to the
church, some very good things happen
with your money. First, you support the
people God has put in your life to train
you. You also support all the efforts of
the church to reach out to others, fund
missionaries, help those in need, and
provide for all sorts of activities to reach
those goals.

Is giving to your church a priority for you?

Talk to your pastor or church treasurer
and ask how the church's money is spent.

Rebuking in Love
Paul's Disagreement With Peter

memory verse

I have been crucified with Christ and I no longer live, but Christ lives in me. The life I live in the body, I live by faith in the Son of God, who loved me and gave himself for me.

Galatians 2:20

"**R**ebuke in love." Somehow those words don't seem to go together. Kind of like other oxymorons, like "jumbo shrimp" or "almost done." How can you rebuke someone and love him at the same time? But this is what God asks us to do when we face problems with other believers.

As Christians we are all still wrestling with our sin nature even though we've been set free from sin. That being the case, there will be times when we have to confront Christian friends— when they gossip to us about others, when they make dating decisions that are scripturally wrong, when they act out of anger instead of love or forgiveness. But do we have to confront them? And if we have to, how do we confront them? Can't we just pray for them? Actually, no. Paul illustrates the point since he dealt with this personally on many occasions. On a return trip to Jerusalem, Peter began backing off from his convictions about Gentiles being allowed equal access in the church. Paul boldly confronted him about it and the matter was resolved. He wrote the Galatians about the incident, not to gloat, but because they were committing the same sin.

One thing is certain: There will be conflict and we have to be involved. We do have a choice, though, in how we handle these situations. This week we're going to look at how to handle conflicts among friends.

Day 1 >
Galatians 2:11-21

How's this for a tense moment? What do you do when Peter and Paul—two of the most famous church leaders of all time—have a disagreement? Paul knew that Peter was being tempted to drift back into old ways, but those old ways jeopardized the gospel. It would have taught people to live by works instead of grace. To Paul, the gospel was worth defending, even though it meant rebuking Peter in public. In Peter's letters we see no hostility in his mention of Paul, so we know that this event didn't ultimately divide them. The real question for you is: Would you confront a friend in order to defend the gospel?

Is the gospel worth jeopardizing a friendship over? Why or why not?

Ask the Father to show you how to balance patience, love, and confrontation.

Day 2 >>
1 Corinthians 5:9-12

How many times have we heard the phrase, "But who am I to judge someone else?" While this is great advice for those outside the church, Paul reminds the Corinthians that if someone claims to be a believer and then lives a lifestyle that is obviously contrary to Scripture, we have an obligation to help bring that person back to a right perspective. It's not an option; it's a command! It's obviously difficult to do this and much easier to ignore the situation. But ignoring it only makes things worse and leaves a Christian brother or sister in the bondage of sin. If we love one another, we must learn to help each other remain faithful—even if that means confronting each other in love when necessary.

What are some reasons we don't confront other believers in love?

Are they valid reasons?

Pray today about any situations where God might have you confront someone in love. Ask for His wisdom in what to say.

Day 3 >>>
James 5:19-20

Some people just like to argue and want to be right all the time. You may know someone like that who seems to confront everyone about everything. But God doesn't tell us to confront others so we can be right and tell them they're wrong. The goal is to save them from the destructive power of sin. If this isn't our goal in rebuking someone, then we don't have the proper attitude. Before you talk to someone else about their problem, ask yourself why you're doing it. Is it really to help them, or is this about you somehow? Remember, we have to rebuke in love—not for our pride, to make a point, or because we don't like them. Check your motives before you confront someone.

Think through the last confrontation you had. Why did you do and say the things you did?

Ask God to fill you with the Holy Spirit in order to be able to rebuke in love rather than for selfish reasons.

Day 4 >>>>
Matthew 18:15-17

When Jesus told us how to confront each other (notice that He knows it will happen among believers), He covered all the bases we've talked about so far. First, He showed us that sin shouldn't go unchecked; it needs to be confronted in the church. Second, He kept talking about brothers. This isn't an academic exercise; it's a chance to love our brother (or sister) and bring him (or her) back into a right relationship with God and the church. Third, by including others in the process, we make sure we're not doing this just out of spite. Having others there who are outside the situation keeps our emotions in check.

Is this process easy? No! But this is the kind of game plan that works.

Have you ever tried this method when dealing with a conflict? How did it go?

Ask the Lord to show you how to walk through each step of the process correctly and prayerfully when confronting someone.

Day 5 >>>>>
Galatians 6:1-5

Confronting our friends is no easy matter. It's messy and can be hurtful. But Paul reminded us that it can also be dangerous. God calls us to help our brothers and sisters get out of sinful patterns and will help us as we help them. But this means that sometimes we will be exposed to the same kind of temptation they've already fallen for. So we have to keep our guard up as we reach out to erring believers; if we don't, we might find ourselves on the receiving end of some corrective discipline. Remember, it's always easier to pull someone down than pull someone up. So be careful. We need to protect ourselves as we help others.

What precautions do you think would be helpful when reaching out to erring friends?

Pray for God's protection and help before you talk to your friends about their sins.

Pray today for anyone you know of in a sin situation.

Faithfulness At Great Cost
Paul's Parting Message to the Ephesians

memory verse

Have nothing to do with godless myths and old wives' tales; rather, train yourself to be godly.

1 Timothy 4:7

I know of a youth group where the students were in the habit of being very emotional during their Wednesday night service. Being emotional is not wrong, but they seemed to get emotional for no reason. The youth minister decided to give them a test. He got up and preached an impassioned talk, then gave an invitation. The altar was full of students! Suddenly he stopped the service and informed them that everything he had just told them was wrong. Not a bit of it was supported by Scripture. They had become emotional about something completely fake.

This danger is not new. At the end of his third missionary journey, Paul was headed back to Jerusalem. On his way he met with the elders of the Ephesian church, where he gave a farewell speech. In this speech, he warned the Ephesians to be aware of those who preach false teachings about God. Paul wouldn't be around anymore to protect them so they had to learn to protect themselves.

We too must be on guard for false teaching. As you continue to mature in your Christian faith, you will probably encounter false teachers. Unless you test the teaching against Scripture, you'll find yourself like that youth group: looking spiritual but having no substance. This week, we're going to learn that if we're going to stay healthy we're going to have to defend our doctrine (our core set of beliefs). God wants us to be passionate about Him, but He also wants us to be wise.

Day 1 >
Acts 20:17-38

Here is the heart of a true shepherd. Paul had always protected those in his church from the destructive influences around them. In this passage he reminded them that demonic forces must be rebuked and that false teachers would try to sneak in through the back door. Paul wouldn't be there to fight them anymore; therefore, he challenged the believers to be alert. False teachers are a tough problem because they don't usually look like bad people; in fact, they might even seem more spiritual than most. But when they subtly begin pushing us to focus on something other than Christ, their true motives can be seen.

Have you ever thought about why you listen to the people you listen to? Are they biblically correct in what they teach?

What standard can you use to tell if they are true teachers or not?

Ask God to provide you with righteous teachers who will steer you straight.

Day 2 >>
2 Timothy 4:1-5

Everyone likes to be told they're right; it's flattering and makes us feel smart. On the other hand, people don't like to be told they're wrong; it makes them feel awkward and uncomfortable. This has always been true, even for members of the early church.

Sometimes God will use people to tell us things that are hard to hear—things that cause us to recognize we're not acting as we should. Instead of running from such teaching (or dismissing it as wrong), we need to be open to it. If we don't, we'll leave ourselves vulnerable to false teachers who tell us exactly what we want to hear. No one is right 100% of the time (not even you), so never assume you don't need someone to challenge you now and then.

How do you respond when you hear hard things that convict you?

Ask God to show you if you have the same problem these church people did.

Day 3 >>>
Revelation 2:1-7

We don't know exactly what the Nicolaitans believed, but it was obviously a false teaching. God commended the Ephesians for testing their teachers. Instead of blindly believing everything they heard, they checked it against Scripture to see if what was being taught was in accordance with the Bible. If it wasn't, they refused to listen. We should trust those God puts in authority over us, but God's Word is the authority over all. What someone says may sound good, but we have to be on guard that we are trusting the words of God not the words of humans. Of course, in order to do that, we need to know what the Word says ourselves!

Are you studying the Word enough that you would be able to spot even a minor false teaching if you heard it?

Day 4 >>>>
1 John 2:18-27

John had a problem. There were people in his church teaching that Jesus was never really flesh and blood—that He just appeared to be. But John had known Jesus and had touched Him personally, so he wrote this letter to clear up any confusion. You may be asking yourself, "How will I know what's right or not; don't these people know more than me? How could I tell them they're wrong?" Good questions. Here John reminded his people that even though he was absent from them, the Holy Spirit was not. So the Spirit resides in you and will help you understand what is right and what is not. That being the case, we need to make sure we are walking in step with the Holy Spirit so we'll know when false teaching arises. You don't have to be a scholar to know the real truth . . . just a Bible-reading, Bible-believing teenager!

Are you walking in step with the Spirit right now? How do you know?

Spend some time thinking through what John said. Do you really believe the Holy Spirit will teach you today?

Day 5 >>>>>
Acts 5:17-33

The ruling Jews at the time were furious with the disciples for talking about Jesus. They tried silencing them time and time again. We live in a much different time today, but many of us can feel the same way when people in our culture tell us not to talk about Jesus. No one in our society wants to hear that Jesus is the only way to heaven, or that they need to be saved from their sins. These are very unpopular ideas. The moment you talk openly about this you may get a reaction similar to the one the disciples got. We can't back down just because people want an inoffensive, watered-down faith. That kind of faith won't save anyone! We should never be ashamed of the gospel.

Do you know the truth well enough to speak openly about it, or do you keep it to yourself? Why?

Ask God to train you so that you can be as bold as the disciples were.

community: The New Testament Church—The Essence of Fellowship

Testimony in Chains
Paul's Arrest

memory verse

Paul replied, "Short time or long— I pray God that not only you but all who are listening to me today may become what I am, except for these chains." **Acts 26:29**

Joni Eareckson Tada has one of those stories that just amazes you. After a diving accident at age 17 left her a quadriplegic, Joni found herself facing a life much different than the one she thought she was going to live. Yet her disability was not strong enough to keep her from serving Christ. She has written more than thirty books, traveled to more than forty countries, and is currently a sought-after speaker as well as an advocate for the disabled. It probably wasn't what Joni planned when she was a teenager, but her ministry has reached millions.

When we find ourselves in difficult circumstances that force us to change our plans, we have two choices we can make. We can either choose to give up, or we can choose to continue to serve Christ— no matter what.

When faced with a particularly difficult time, the Apostle Paul chose to serve Christ. In Acts 24—26, we find the story of Paul's imprisonment and trials. Paul could have given up at any point—he faced some pretty tough circumstances. But he stayed true to his calling and continued to preach the message of Jesus Christ. He couldn't see it all then, but he knew God had plans for Paul even in jail. How would you have responded?

This week we're going to face one of the hardest questions of life: How do we serve God when things don't go our way?

Day 1 >

Acts 24:24-27; 25:9-12; 26:24-32

So what do you do if you're Paul and you find yourself in jail for more than two years? Pout? Sulk? Get angry? Paul may have had days when he did all of these things, but for the most part we know what he did while in prison. He did the same thing he was doing before he was arrested—he preached about Jesus. Paul had been called to spread the name of Jesus and so no matter where he found himself he continued doing just that. When things don't go as we planned, or we don't get to serve the way we wanted, it's easy to throw in the towel. But then we miss out on all the unexpected blessings God is sending us. Prison couldn't stop Paul. Are you letting anything stop you?

If your life dreams never come true, will you still serve Christ as best as you can?

Spend some time today praying about anything hindering you from serving Christ with everything you have.

Day 2 >>

Philippians 1:12-18

Paul appears to be an optimist. He wasn't getting to do what he wanted. (I'm sure he would have rather been planting churches or preaching in a marketplace.) Instead, he was in prison and it didn't look like he'd be getting out anytime soon. But Paul saw the bigger picture. Even his imprisonment was advancing the gospel. The letters of Philippians, Colossians, Ephesians, and Philemon were all written from jail. These letters have been helping believers for almost 2,000 years. I'm sure letter writing wasn't his favorite form of ministry, but God used it. Even when life doesn't go as you wanted, God can use you greatly.

If God gave you a plan that was different than the one you wanted, would you follow it anyway?

Think back on some things in your past that you didn't enjoy. Ask the Father to show you how He has used these events for good in your life—or someone else's.

Day 3 >>>
Hebrews 11:32-39

When bad things happen I wonder, "Did I do something wrong? Is God punishing me?" Satan will tell us this whether it's true or not. When we face setbacks in our plans, we may wonder if we really have God's blessing. But look at the list in today's passage. While God blessed many people in the Old Testament, the list breaks mid-verse and talks of others who had a rougher time. But all of them are commended, regardless of their circumstances. Just because you are struggling in your attempts to serve doesn't mean God has forgotten you. Don't look at your circumstances to determine whether God is with you; rely on His Word!

Do you find security in your circumstances . . . or in God's Word? (Think back to your last crisis to find out.)

Ask God to give you strength to endure when things seem confusing.

Day 4 >>>>
Psalm 42

If the Bible is anything, it is honest. Some may picture the saints of old as perfect men who calmly endured affliction; but the Scriptures speak otherwise. The psalms show the raw emotion of those walking through tough times. Here the psalmist declared He would still hope in God even though the reasons he used to be joyful had collapsed. Why was he so confident? Because even though his circumstances had changed, his God had not. The God he worshipped when things were good is the God he would continue to worship even though it was hard. This kind of worship requires a choice to believe despite feelings. The results might surprise you; this woeful writer found not only comfort from God, but a chance to encourage people like us thousands of years later.

community: The New Testament Church—The Essence of Fellowship

Think about a time when you chose to worship even when you didn't feel like it.

Write your own psalm to the Lord today below. Above all, be honest with God.

Day 5 >>>>>
Acts 24:24-27

OK, let's say you're Paul. You know you're supposed to be out spreading the Word of God, but you're stuck in jail. The guy holding you prisoner wants a bribe. You could easily get your hands on the money since you've got a lot of friends who want you out. What do you do? I'm sure Paul could have found a way to bribe Festus, yet he stayed put for two years. Why? Because the ends don't justify the means. God is in control and He won't ask us to violate our faith even if we have a logical reason for doing so. God hasn't forgotten you and He will take care of you no matter what your circumstances are. Be patient! Even though you may not understand what's going on, God does; your job is to continue to trust.

Have you ever rationalized a sin because you thought you had a good reason?

Why was that the wrong thing to do?

Decide today to react in a godly manner instead of a worldly manner when it comes to making tough decisions.

An Indirect Path: Paul Sails For Rome

memory verse

But the centurion wanted to spare Paul's life and kept them from carrying out their plan. He ordered those who could swim to jump overboard first and get to land.

Acts 27:43

Fairs are fun. Dangerous, but fun. Every year I looked forward to going to the fair because I would get to ride the Scrambler. Have you ever ridden the Scrambler? It flings you left and right, back and forth, all while moving in a huge circle. It was fun . . . unless you had eaten a funnel cake right before you got on.

A lot of times our Christian journey seems like the Scrambler. You expect it to be a calm journey that moves predictably from one stage to the next. But what you actually get is a sudden move to the left, then to the right, then forward, then backward. In Acts 27:27-28:6, Paul went through a journey sort of like this. Amazingly, he endures a huge storm, a shipwreck, and a snake attack.

Paul thought that Rome would be his big obstacle, only to find out that his journey getting there would be just as eventful. But God was in control, and He is in control even when we can't discern the reasons. Our job is to stick close to Him, hold on tight, and trust Him even though we don't always understand where we're going.

Through it all, we can serve Christ along the way. So get ready, the Christian journey might end up being a lot more exciting than you thought. Oh, and you might want to skip that funnel cake.

Day 1 >
Acts 27:27-28:6

Who says the Bible isn't exciting? One thing is sure: Following God is a greater adventure than anything else. If we're bored, it's probably not His fault. Paul probably wasn't expecting all this when he wanted to go to Rome, but here again we see him serving God wherever he was. All the men on the ship respect his decisions even though he was one of the prisoners. He ended up being able to witness to the locals and the governor. It may not have been on the itinerary, but Paul made the most of his circumstances. Life probably doesn't happen according to plan, but you can still make the most of every opportunity. But you have to choose to do so.

How can you make the most of opportunities today?

Spend some time praying that God would prepare you for whatever lies ahead today.

Day 2 >>
1 Samuel 17:32-37

This passage is from famous David and Goliath incident. (If you've never read this entire story, read chapter 17). Here's the background: David had been anointed king over Israel but had been tending sheep for years. He wouldn't actually get to be king for a few years more. God was using this time to prepare David. In this passage, he said he was not afraid of Goliath because of two incidents with a bear and a lion. Imagine being David. He was supposed to be king and he ended up fighting a bear. "What does this have to do with being king?" he may have wondered. Well, on this particular day he found out. Even when your life seems to make no sense at all, trust that God is doing things we won't understand—until later.

What does this story tell you about God?

Decide today to trust God regardless of how your circumstances appear.

Day 3 >>>
Exodus 13:20-22; 40:34-38

If you were an Israelite during the Exodus and wondered whether God was with you, you could check the tabernacle. You could actually see God's presence day or night over the tabernacle. You may wish God would do that today. Wouldn't that make it easier to know He's always with us? True, but remember that even though they could see the presence of God with them, He led them in a way they didn't understand at all. To them it looked like that cloud was leading them on a wild goose chase. The point was to teach them to follow, no matter what. God is trying to teach us the

community: The New Testament Church—The Essence of Fellowship

same thing. Instead of following a cloud, we get to follow the Spirit Himself. Sometimes the route will seem odd, but our call is still the same: "Follow Me."

Try to put yourself in the Israelites' shoes. After 27 years, would you find it easy or hard to keep following? Why?

Ask God to lead you by His Spirit today. Commit to follow Him no matter what.

Day 4 >>>>
Acts 18:1-6

Some people think if you're spiritual, you can pick up poisonous snakes—and even be bitten—and not be killed. Yes, this is one of the passages they cite to prove it. But that's not really the point here. Paul didn't go out of his way to find a snake to play with. God had His hand on Paul and used this incident to open a door for sharing the gospel. Paul now had a chance to tell them that he wasn't a god but that he knew the real One. God doesn't recreate miracles for everyone, but His purposes remain unchanged. You don't need snakes to prove you're holy; you can prove that by staying true to God's purposes and living according to His plans.

Have you ever seen someone take Scripture and use it out of context (like using this passage to mean that if we are super spiritual poisonous snakes won't affect us)?

Day 5 >>>>>

2 Corinthians 11:21-33

Paul's life and writings shaped Western civilization as we know it. Of course, God was in charge of that, and without Christ Paul wouldn't have amounted to much. But let's not forget Satan in all of this. We have an enemy who seeks to destroy us every day. The list of hardships in this passage indicates that those of us who want to serve Christ wholeheartedly have a fight on our hands. Remember: Satan doesn't win when we follow Christ—no matter what happens! It might be painful, difficult, dangerous, and trying, but our circumstances cannot stop us if we truly rely on God. Paul's life is a testimony to that fact. Are you letting your circumstances stop you from being like Paul?

What do we learn about God's wisdom and control through this passage?

Ask God to use you as He used Paul, regardless of the path it requires you take.

Every Opportunity
Paul Preaches In Prison

memory verse

"Therefore I want you to know that God's salvation has been sent to the Gentiles, and they will listen!"
Acts 28:28

God uses us in amazing ways. Many times you don't see it coming. A few years ago I was preaching at a summer camp on a college campus. One night after giving the invitation, I went backstage to help counsel students who had responded to the invitation. But I stopped by the restroom on the way. As I entered the bathroom a young guy followed me in. After a few awkward pleasantries, he said, "I've never really been saved before." He told me this in the bathroom! (I definitely didn't see that one coming!) After we walked out of the restroom I had the privilege of introducing him to Christ.

Opportunities to serve and share Christ are everywhere. The trick is learning to see them. Once we realize that we can literally serve Christ 24/7, things get interesting. When we left Paul he was just getting to Rome. In Acts 28 we find out that, just as before, he was going to find himself in jail for a long time. For some people, this would have been a huge letdown. But for Paul? No problem. He didn't allow pesky details like imprisonment keep him from faithfully sharing the gospel every day.

This week we're going to try to follow Paul's lead and learn how to take advantage of every opportunity we find to serve Christ.

Day 1 >

Acts 28:16-30

How's this for dedication? Paul was under house arrest awaiting trial and couldn't go out to tell others about Jesus. I might have given up at this point—or at least felt sorry for myself. Paul didn't have time for sulking. This was another obstacle with a God-sized solution. If he couldn't go to them, get them to come to him!

Sometimes we won't get the opportunities we want to serve God, but opportunities are around us nonetheless. Paul decided to serve no matter what the circumstances and therefore had a huge impact for God's Kingdom. When we decide to use every circumstance, we too will see God moving in great ways.

Think about some creative ways to share Christ during activities you will be involved in today.

Ask God to give you the kind of dedication that drove Paul to use every opportunity for Christ.

Day 2 >>

Ephesians 5:15-17

We should never forget that we have an enemy who wants us to waste opportunities. Verse 16 reminds us that the days in which we live are evil. Most of the time we skip over phrases like this. But a spiritual war is really going on and you're involved whether you like it or not. As we have opportunities to share the gospel, serve, and love others, we will also be under temptation to ignore those opportunities. This is a spiritual attack we must recognize! If you expect to be tempted, you will be more prepared to fight off those enemy attacks.

What are the temptations Satan uses in your life most often to keep you from serving Christ?

How can you best defend yourself against those temptations?

Go back to Ephesians 6:10-18 and pray through your spiritual armor today.

Day 3 >>>
Hebrews 3:12-15

I think procrastination is something everyone wrestles with. If an assignment is due on Friday, we can wait until at least . . . Thursday night . . . right? The problem with procrastinating spiritually is that some opportunities only come along once. The writer of Hebrews knew this and urged his readers to do what God asked them to do immediately . . . not Friday. If we procrastinate, we may lose the opportunity forever. We may also lose spiritual ground as sin sinks deeper into our daily routine. We have to be relentless about taking opportunities when they arise because you are not guaranteed to ever have them again! This even goes for talking to your best friend about Jesus. You may never get another chance. Use the one you have!

What spiritual opportunity have you missed because of procrastination?

How can you prepare yourself to seize opportunities today?

Day 4 >>>>

Philippians 3:12-13

Most of us feel more guilt about the opportunities we've wasted than joy about the ones we've seized. How do we turn things around and put ourselves in the joy column? When we rely on ourselves to go out and serve, we can only do so much. Paul relied on God's power instead of his own; that way, no matter where he found himself, he knew he was right where God wanted him. God is not sending you on a solo mission; He wants you to lean on Him. Don't view today as a test but as a joint mission. Let God empower you and see what happens.

Think back to the last thing you did for God. Whose power did you rely on?

What were the results?

Ask God to help you rely on Him instead of yourself today.

Day 5 >>>>>
Acts 28:30-31

Kind of an odd way to end a book, isn't it? Luke leaves us with this picture of Paul preaching in chains in Rome. But this wasn't the end for Paul. We know that he ultimately got out of jail and continued to travel and preach the gospel before being re-arrested, re-tried, and ultimately executed for his faith. Why end this way? God is the main character in this story, not Peter or Paul, so it's fitting that Luke finished his book with Paul faithfully spreading the gospel from his imprisonment. God fulfilled His promise to bring Paul to Rome, and after the Book of Acts ended God continued to use Paul. As we have seen throughout the Book of Acts, nothing can stop the advance of the gospel.

What have you learned about God through the Book of Acts?

Spend some time reflecting on the whole book and writing down what has stood out the most.

One in Christ
Paul's Letter to the Ephesians, Part 1

memory verse

Consequently, you are no longer foreigners and aliens, but fellow citizens with God's people and members of God's household.

Ephesians 2:19

Have you ever wondered how you got into your family? I have. I'm completely different from my parents and fairly different from my brother. So how did we all end up in the same family? We have one major thing in common: our last name. Whether we like it or not, we are all in the same family. Different as we are, we all have the same blood linking us.

The same is true for the Church. The New Testament Church was made up of an assortment of very different kinds of people who up until now had lived separate lives. What could possibly connect all these people? They now had the same bloodline: the blood of Jesus. Because of Jesus' sacrificial death, everyone who places faith in Christ—regardless of their race, gender, or ethnicity—is a part of the Church. When Jesus rose again, He began to build His family. His Church was composed of people He loved and who loved Him. But His family would also love each other. While in prison in Rome, Paul wrote a letter to the church in Ephesus to help them understand their common lineage in Christ. Through this letter, Paul tried to help the Ephesians see that all people are welcomed into the church family regardless of their differences.

This also holds true for your church. Wildly different people are all included: men and women, rich and poor, popular and unpopular. This week, we'll look at who makes up the church—your church—and how to live in it.

Day 1 >
Ephesians 2:11-22

I grew up in the South where just about everyone was a Christian (or at least pretended to be), so I've always felt comfortable in church. It's hard for me to think about being far away from God since I've heard about Him all my life. But here Paul reminded us that no matter how familiar we are with God or how long we've known Him, we used to be far away from Him. Literally, we were like aliens to Him . . . strangers! Until we were saved, we were completely cut off from God. That's why this is such a great passage. We're in! Even though we don't deserve to be in the church, through Jesus we can be.

Take some time today, and think about what it would be like if you didn't know Jesus. Spend some time thanking Him today for making you a part of His family.

Day 2 >>
Ephesians 2:17-22

I know; I know...same passage from yesterday. But there's always more to a passage if we'll spend enough time with it. Look at the following phrase: "in Him." It shows up twice in verses 21-22. Paul was telling us about the foundation of the Church. He was showing us that we aren't just a club or a group of people who happen to like being moral and singing on Sundays. He reminded us that the core of who we are is the person of Jesus. Our lives are a temple where Jesus lives. Everything we believe should be based on Him. If it's not about Jesus, it's not church. But also note that you're mentioned in this verse. Verse 22 says that you, too, are a part of this building program. You are an active part of this church that's been growing for almost 2,000 years.

Why do you go to church?

Would your life be different if you didn't? How?

Ask God to show you how He can be the foundation of your life.

Day 3 >>>
1 Corinthians 12:14-31

There are hundreds of parts in our bodies. There are so many that I don't even know most of them. But I'm glad to have them all, and I'd rather not lose any. Each one of them has a particular function and is necessary for the whole body to work properly. The same is true in the church. Growing up, I used to think that the only real jobs in a church were pastor, youth minister, and music minister. But everyone—yes, even you—has a place, not just the people on the church staff. God

has made you to be a vital part of your church. You have unique gifts that no one else has, and God is intent on using you as an active part of that church body.

What's your role in your church?

Where are some places you can be actively involved in your church as a teenager?

Day 4 >>>>
Ephesians 3:1-4

You have probably been on some sort of team at one time or another in your life. Chances are, there were some people on it that you didn't always get along with, but they were still your teammates. If you were on a football team, others were your teammates because they also played football. If you were on a drama team, others were your teammates because they also performed drama. There's always some unifying base on which a team is built.

The same thing is true with the church. For us, the thing we all have in common is our relationship to Jesus. No matter how different we are, all Christians are our brothers and sisters. This means we can't exclude or ignore them just because they don't go to our church, and we can't shun them just because they may not be our favorite people. We are on the same team with them—the Church of Jesus Christ.

Do you ever exclude some believers because they aren't like you?

What are some ways you could reach out to them instead?

Day 5 >>>>>
Romans 10:12-13

The Birmingham Civil Rights Institute chronicles the battle for racial equality that was waged on the streets of my city. The same kind of racism existed between the Jews and Gentiles in Scripture. Jesus broke down the barriers between them. The Bible is filled with verses reminding us that God shows no favoritism. Even more, no matter how different we seem to be from one another, there's one thing we all have in common: our sin. Everyone needs Jesus—everyone. So there's never a time when prejudice is justified. We all have a common problem, and we all have a common Savior. Are we ready and willing to accept everyone into the church? Jesus is, and because He is, we must be, too.

Think back on how and when you became a Christian. Thank God for not excluding you. Ask Christ to help you not exclude others, especially those who are different from you.

Equipping for Ministry
Paul's Letter to the Ephesians, Part 2

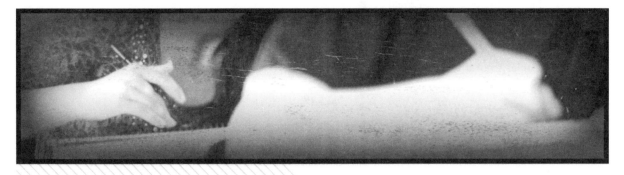

memory verse

Instead, speaking the truth in love, we will in all things grow up into him who is the Head, that is, Christ. **Ephesians 4:15**

I did not enjoy my time in high school English class. I had a teacher who was always making me revise my essays. She was never satisfied with my first tries, and she rarely gave out compliments. Ugh! I don't even like thinking about it. But, looking back years later, I have to say that it was probably one of the best classes I ever had, and she turned out to be one of the best teachers I ever had. Why? Because she actually challenged me to learn something . . . and I did. In fact, I learned a lot.

Teachers aren't there to be our buddies but to make sure we learn things we may not even want to learn. Without them, we'd never become the people God wants us to be.

Still writing from prison Paul tried to help the Ephesians understand the different kinds of leadership in the church. He was helping them see that certain people were called to teach them and to lead them. If they were going to grow in faith, they would have to

follow these people and work toward growing as Christians.

We tend to view learning from our leaders as I did my English teacher: "Do I have to do this?" How many sermons have we dutifully sat through without actually learning anything? But just as I did with my English teacher, if we submit to doing the work, we'll find that we can accomplish more than before. This week, we're going to look at how our pastors and teachers help equip us for life.

Day 1 >

Ephesians 4:11-16

Have you ever had the thought that, for people to get saved, they had to show up at church? It makes sense, doesn't it? I mean, the pastor can explain it so much better than us, can't he? This kind of thinking can get us into trouble. According to this passage, God has given you pastors and teachers to prepare you to go share the gospel, not just bring people to church. A pastor's job is to teach you; your job is to use that training out in the real world. If we accept this fact, then church becomes our training ground—our home base from which we learn and grow—so we can fight the real battles out in the world.

Do you expect the ministers in your church to do all the serious spiritual work in your church? Is that a biblical idea?

How would your experience be different if you saw church as a training ground and its ministers as your teachers and equippers?

Day 2 >>

Ephesians 4:11-16

Time for a reality check. Do you really want to grow spiritually? Honestly? Everyone needs to grow up spiritually, but this doesn't happen automatically. You can show up at church for the next 10 years

community: The New Testament Church—The Essence of Fellowship

and not grow one bit unless you choose to. But if you really do want to grow, ask yourself how you are accomplishing that goal—or how you can start to do so. You may already be doing the right things but not really putting any effort into it; you know, kind of like going through the motions. Or there may be things you need to change. Get honest about whether you really want to grow spiritually, because no one can help you grow if you don't want to.

Spend some time today asking yourself this question: Do I really want to grow?

In your prayer time today, ask God to give you a real desire to grow, and ask Him to show you ways to do so.

Day 3 >>>
1 Peter 3:15-16

This has always been one of those extra-challenging Scripture passages for me. If you've ever gotten into a spiritual debate that is way over your head, you know how hard defending your faith can be. The thing to remember is that everyone starts somewhere. And no one expects you to have all the answers. (I certainly don't have them all.) But you should be able to hold your own about your beliefs. Instead of saying, "Let's go ask my pastor," you need to be able to explain to others why you are a Christian and why you believe what you do. This requires some hard work, since you have to stop and think about what you believe. Have you ever done that?

Spend some time thinking about what you believe. Ask God to help you understand your relationship with Him.

Day 4 >>>>
Galatians 1:13-24

Did you catch verse 18? Three years! After Paul got saved he didn't just take off on his first missionary journey. Even though he was one of the smartest Jews around, he needed to be trained and that wasn't a quick process. He spent three years learning about Christ before he went to teach anyone anything. If Paul needed that kind of training, we do as well. After you get saved, there is a lot to learn, and you won't learn it overnight. So cut yourself some slack; you're not supposed to understand everything yet. But you should get to work. We have a lot to learn, and we need to be as diligent about learning as Paul.

Are you putting yourself in places where you can learn from those who have been walking with Jesus longer than you? If not, what is your reason for not doing so?

community: The New Testament Church—The Essence of Fellowship

Pray today for God to help you grow by learning what He wants you to learn today.

Day 5 >>>>>
Luke 10:1-23

"Aren't you coming with us?" I bet that was the first thing on these guys' minds when Jesus sent them out. They had been following Jesus and watching Him do miracles, but now Jesus was sending them out on a solo flight. And that's very different! Being equipped isn't just sitting and listening; it's experiencing ministry. Part of your training will actually be witnessing to someone, going on short-term mission trips, and serving in your church. You may not feel ready yet, but no one ever feels as though they are really ready. Be willing to take the opportunities God throws your way so you can continue growing.

Do you avoid any situation in which you aren't perfectly comfortable?

Could you be missing out on something God is asking you to experience?

Look for a ministry opportunity God is asking you to try today. Do it even if you don't feel completely comfortable yet. Ask God to give you courage and teach you something new. You have to stretch in order to grow!

A Unified Church
Paul's Letter to the Philippians

memory verse
Do nothing out of selfish ambition or vain conceit, but in humility consider others better than yourselves.

Philippians 2:3

As I'm writing this devotional, Ukrainians are filling the streets of Kiev to protest the fraudulent elections there. They want the truth, and in peaceful protest tens of thousands of them have continued to march and demand change. It's a powerful image. It challenges me anytime I see a large group of people coming together for a common purpose. When this happens, it shows that something is more important than all their other differences . . . something that transcends personal ambitions.

God is trying to build that same spirit of unity in us. One of the things Paul stressed in the prison epistles of Philippians and Ephesians is the unity of the church. But how do such different people act in concert? By imitating Christ and following the example He set. What an incredible unified body we would be if everyone in the church were to follow this example. One day this will be a reality, and we're all going to see it. But until then, God is busy building that unity among all of us.

We're going to take a look this week at the unity of the church and find out that God truly desires for us to put aside our differences and come together as one universal church. It's going to require some changes on all of our parts, but the result will be a sight that will do more than simply confound corrupt politicians; it will change the whole world.

Philippians 2:1-4

Being one in purpose with others isn't always the easiest thing to do. Most of us would rather everyone else agree with us! But Paul didn't just command the Philippians to be unified; he told them that their unity was a sign they have been changed. If we have really experienced Christ, we should be changed. We really weren't able to show unity before, but now that we've been changed, our unity is one of the signs that Christ is moving in us. If we can't be unified with other believers, our spirituality is in question. How do you interact with other believers? Can you get along with other Christians? Is working with other believers a priority for you? The Holy Spirit will help you when this is hard.

Think on all the things mentioned in Verse 1, and thank Christ for those gifts.

Pray that God would show you how to share those gifts with other believers today.

Day 2 >>

Philippians 2:5-11

I like my life. More to the point, I like how I live my life: however I want to. But when you have a family or live with other people, you find out very quickly that you have to make some changes if everyone is going to get along. Compromise is necessary to make life work in community. Jesus thought it was worth the price. See all the things he had to do to bring us into the family? He thought it was worth laying aside His glory—just for us. If Jesus was willing to do that for us, then we need to be willing to make sacrifices for others. It's not always easy (it certainly wasn't for Jesus), but it does bring new life.

What areas of your life will you have to change to live in unity with other believers? Are you willing to make those sacrifices?

Ask God to show you how to do that through His power—not your own.

Day 3 >>>
John 17:20-23

How's this for a startling statement: Jesus prayed that, as believers, we would have the same kind of unity that exists in God Himself! He is Father, Son, and Holy Spirit yet still one God. It's a mystery to be sure, but that's the model for how unified He wants us to be. If we are able to live in that kind of unity, it shows people that something supernatural is present. Disunity is natural—even expected (kind of like how you and your siblings sometimes get on each other's nerves). So imagine how stunned people would be if we as Christians all lived in unity. It is possible through Christ, but only if we are willing.

If you feel that you are not living in unity with other believers, what do you think is holding you back?

What are you doing to clear the obstacles away?

Ask God to enable you to overcome anything that would keep you from this kind of intimacy with others.

Day 4 >>>>
Revelation 7:9-10

Some denominations think they'll be the only ones in heaven. I have a feeling heaven will seem a bit more crowded than expected. God's plan is for unity among all believers. But how do we unify all the different denominations? It's a lot of work to maintain unity just in my church, much less all churches. Is it really that big a deal? In this passage, we see the end of time. Here is a picture of the church as God intends it to be, believers united from all over the world praising Him together. If this is the plan, we should be working on our small part of that unity as best we can.

Begin thinking about what it will look like in Heaven for all of us to finally be worshipping together.

What's keeping you from working together with believers whom you know from other church denominations?

Day 5 >>>>>

Ephesians 4:1-6

One of the reasons it's hard to be unified with other believers is that we seem to be so different. Different churches, different personalities, even different opinions on minor issues. So how can we expect to get along? Paul reminds the Ephesians that, while they do share a lot of differences, they also have a lot of similarities, and these are much greater than their differences. We all have the same God, we were baptized into the same body of believers, and we have the same Holy Spirit. No matter who we are and what church we attend, if we are Christians, we are all saved the same way: by the grace of God. No one deserves to be here more than anyone else because we all came through the same door. Once we recognize this, it's a lot harder to throw up walls between each other since, at our cores, we are all the same where it really counts: We're children of God.

What are some of the things that divide you from other believers?

Are they valid reasons for not being united with them?

Prayer
Paul's First Letter to Timothy, Part 1

memory verse

I urge, then, first of all, that requests, prayers, intercession and thanksgiving be made for everyone—for kings and all those in authority, that we may live peaceful and quiet lives in all godliness and holiness.

1 Timothy 2:1-2

In the past decade, we've seen some of the closest elections in American history. With such small margins of victory, few would deny that every vote is important. No one can honestly say it doesn't matter if they vote. Voting is the right and privilege of American citizens. No matter who you are, once you turn 18, you get that right and the power that comes with it.

As believers in Jesus Christ, we have something even more powerful (and you don't have to wait until you're 18). God tells us that our prayers are incredibly powerful—a stronger force than you've ever dreamed. Combined with those of other Christians, our prayers are an amazing force in the world.

Paul knew the importance of prayer. In his first letter to Timothy, written while he was imprisoned in Rome, Paul was nearing the end of his life. Looking back on his ministry, Paul knew unmistakably that the prayers of the churches were the foundation of his spiritual successes. He wanted Timothy and all of his churches to never forget how tremendously powerful the prayers of the saints are.

This week, we're going to look at both the prayers of the church and our personal prayer lives. It could be that you've never really thought about your prayer life; maybe it's just something you do. But with a force this powerful, we should expect the supernatural.

Day 1 >

1 Timothy 2:1-8

It seems that everyone has a political opinion today, but politicians come and go. What doesn't change is God's plan for the world and your role in that plan. Believe it or not, you are very important in bringing God's plans to fruition. When you pray for government leaders, for the advancement of the gospel in other parts of the world, or for Satan's plans to be defeated, you are making a real impact. God could do this on His own, but He's not going to. He wants to use you as well. That's His plan, so your prayers are incredibly important. They can have worldwide impact! That means we need to be diligent in our prayers for what's going on outside our small circle of friends.

What are some global concerns of the church that you can pray about today?

Ask God to give you a bigger picture of how your prayers affect the world around you.

Day 2 >>

James 5:13-18

Do you ever feel like your prayers bounce off the ceiling—that God might listen to Billy Graham, your pastor, or someone really holy, but not someone like you? I think most of us feel that way. In today's

community: The New Testament Church—The Essence of Fellowship

passage, James encouraged the people in his church to pray—all of them. In the Old Testament, the Jews had their own version of Billy Graham named Elijah. God answered his prayers (you can read about it in 1 Kings 17-18). But James said that Elijah was just a man like you and me. And God wants to answer your prayers in the same way. The question for us is whether we want to be righteous, like Elijah. If we do, there's no reason why we can't see that kind of power in our prayer lives!

When was the last time you saw God answer prayer in your life?

Pray in faith today about something only God could accomplish.

Day 3 >>>
Ephesians 6:18-20

By now, you've probably picked up on the fact that the Christian life is not just about you; it's about us. If that's true, then our prayer lives should reflect the fact. In this passage Paul instructed us to have each other's backs as we fight spiritual battles each day. We must pray for one another if we want to succeed. Case in point: Paul asked the Ephesians to pray that he would preach with boldness. Can you believe that? Did Paul really need any help? Apparently he did, and he relied on his church family for that help. In the same way, we need to be praying for our church family every day, asking God to protect us, help us grow, and use us for His glory.

Do your prayers typically revolve only around you?

How can you change that?

Who are you praying for daily?

Day 4 >>>>
Ephesians 6:18

I know you read this verse yesterday, but think about it for a minute. Paul told us to pray with all kinds of prayer. Have you ever thought about the fact that there are many ways to pray? I usually get stuck in a rut, such as, "God, could you help me with . . ." Paul reminded us to use different types of prayer. Richard J. Foster wrote a book outlining 21 different kinds such as intercessory prayer, healing prayer, prayers of suffering, and many, many more. Today, do something different for your prayer time. You could spend the whole time thanking God for all the things you have that you can see. You could go outside and praise God for His creation. You could sit in silence and just listen, not asking for anything. You could just pray for others' needs today. Let's put this verse into practice by experimenting today. (It's legal, I promise. Try it out!)

Day 5 >>>>>
1 Thessalonians 5:17

How's that for a quick memory verse? In typical Paul fashion, he gave some final instructions to the Thessalonians and included this command. But doesn't this sound unrealistic? How can you pray all the time? Wouldn't you run into things with your eyes closed? Actually, Paul meant that we should be in an active relationship with God so that we can communicate with Him whenever and wherever we are. Awhile back, I started trying out flash prayers while in public. Instead of having a formal prayer time, I kept my eyes open and prayed quick two-second prayers for people I saw. I prayed, "God, show me how to encourage that person," or "God, I pray You'd help her; she looks upset." You can do this hundreds of times a day, and it helps keep you focused throughout the day. It really is possible. Give it a try!

Do you talk to God only during your quiet time? Why?

Ask God to show you places you can pray for others throughout your day.

Qualified Leaders
Paul's First Letter to Timothy, Part 2

memory verse

Beyond all question, the mystery of godliness is great: He appeared in a body, was vindicated by the Spirit, was seen by angels, was preached among the nations, was believed on in the world, was taken up in glory. **1 Timothy 3:16**

Televangelists bug me. Have you ever actually listened to these guys? Some are great men of God, to be sure, but many are charlatans with a lot of charisma and very little depth. Many are masters at bending Scripture to suit their needs. It seems that few of these men are interested in truly teaching people the Word of God; most of them seem more interested in people's money.

Unfortunately, from time to time leaders creep into the church who mirror the lack of character displayed by some televangelists. It's a problem that was around long before television. Paul understood the danger. In his last letters he left clear commands about how to evaluate people who want to be leaders in the church.

False leaders have always been a threat to the Church. But God is faithful to send us qualified leaders who can truly teach the Bible and instruct us to be better followers of Christ. This week, we're going to look at the qualifications for being a leader in the church. We need to know this so we can weed out the false teachers from those who can really help us. We also need to know because God may call you to be a leader.

Day 1 >

1 Timothy 3:1-15

Some people seem to be natural-born leaders. But being a leader means more than being in charge. In order to be a good leader, especially a spiritual leader, you must have certain qualifications. In today's passage, Paul described some of those qualifications. Almost all have to do with character. God is more interested in you being a man or woman of God than a great speaker or a popular person. Why? Because talent can be misused. If you are a godly person, you will lead well because you have the character to use your gifts positively.

Have you ever wanted to lead? Why or why not?

Take a personal inventory of your character based on today's verses. Which of these traits do you need to work on?

Ask God today to continue shaping your character.

Day 2 >>

1 Timothy 1:3-7

For most of us, leading others is not on our to-do lists. The thought may even scare you. To be honest, it can be scary to take on the responsibility of leading others. But God always needs good leaders, and He may call you to be one. God will sometimes choose people who never thought of leading to be the best leaders of all. Saul never asked to be a leader. At his coronation, he was so scared he was hiding in some luggage. (Read the story in 1 Samuel 10:17-27) Sounds like some leader, huh? If God calls you to lead, you need to take the challenge and not give in to fear. You may not feel up to it, but if He calls you, He will equip you. Trust Him and don't fear!

Do you feel like a leader today? Why or why not?

Pray that God would reveal His plan for your role as a leader in His Kingdom.

Day 3 >>>
1 Timothy 3:6-7

Some people have "leadership material" written all over them, but they still may not be ready to lead others. Today, Paul reminds us that new converts aren't prepared for leadership yet. This may seem odd, since new converts are usually some of the most excited Christians we know. Why shouldn't we let them use that energy? While they may be sincere and excited, they don't have the maturity to handle everything just yet. You may have a lot of passion but still need some time before God uses you as a leader on a larger scale. Also, Paul told us that real

community: The New Testament Church—The Essence of Fellowship

leaders are people who are respected by outsiders as well as by those in the church. Good leaders love people no matter where they are or what they are doing.

How is your reputation among non-Christians?

Do they know that you love them and can interact with them even if you don't live like they do?

Ask God to mold your character today so you can lead others.

Day 4 >>>>
Psalm 51

Leaders aren't perfect. In fact, if they look perfect, there's probably something wrong! The Old Testament is filled with examples of godly people who made very sinful decisions. Moses killed a man. Davidcommitted adultery and murder. Abraham lied about his wife. But, as in these cases, making mistakes doesn't disqualify us from service. David wrote today's passage after he made a huge mistake and was confronted about it. The true test of a leader is his ability to own up to his sin, accept the consequences, and make changes to prevent it from happening again. Leaders are held to a higher standard, but we should always leave room for mistakes and repentance. After all, isn't that how we want them to treat us?

Have you ever had a leader disappoint you? How did he or she respond? How did you respond?

Ask God to show you how to forgive your leaders when they make mistakes.

Day 5 >>>>>
Galatians 6:6

As a kid, I often forgot about the giver once I got the gift. As soon as that wrapping paper was off, I was totally focused on that new toy, but I wasn't very grateful. God has been good to provide us with lots of teachers and leaders to show us how to follow Him. God also wants those leaders to be encouraged as they teach us. One of the ways we can encourage our leaders is to make sure we let them know how much we appreciate their leadership in our lives. Telling them how we are growing, reminding them that they are really helping us, and respecting their leadership are all ways we can give something back to those who give leadership to us. Let's not forget the ones who give so much to us.

How can you encourage your pastor and other church leaders today?

Spend some time praying for them and asking God to bless their ministries.

community: The New Testament Church—The Essence of Fellowship

The Bible
Paul's Second Letter to Timothy, Part 1

memory verse

All Scripture is God-breathed and is useful for teaching, rebuking, correcting and training in righteousness, so that the man of God may be thoroughly equipped for every good work.
2 Timothy 3:16-17

Authority is one of those words we don't particularly like. Who wants to listen to authority? But think about what life would be like without authority in our country. With no laws, people would do whatever they wanted. Imagine driving with no traffic lights or stop signs. It would be chaos. Everyone needs a foundation, something solid to stand on, something that won't break in the midst of problems. Because of their belief in Jesus alone as God, the early Church was written off as a bunch of religious kooks.

Our culture asks Christians, "What makes you right and everyone else wrong?" It's an honest question.

The answer is we don't base our lives on our opinions or our desires. We base our lives on the Word of God. As Paul trained leaders for his churches, he spelled out why the Bible is so important for Christians. The Bible is God's unchanging foundation that shows us what truth is. It's the authority of our lives.

When God tells us through Scripture that something is right, it's right. We know this because God inspired His Word and made sure it was passed down to us accurately without changing for thousands of years. The foundation of the church is also the foundation of our lives. This week, we're going to look at the place Scripture has in our daily lives.

Day 1 >

2 Timothy 3:14-17; 2 Peter 1:20-21

Time for another reality check. You may have been reading the Bible for most of your life, or maybe you just picked it up. Either way, here's the question: Do you really believe this is God's Word? Not just rules, not just someone's opinion, and not just an old book. But if you really believe it is God's Word, do you obey it? If we believe in it, then we should be striving to do what it says. But you need to know for yourself. This really is God's Word, but you'll never make it a part of your life unless you firmly believe it is what it says it is. Put it to the test, and find out that it really is a firm place to put your faith.

How would you respond to someone who said the Bible was just another book?

Think about an experience you've had when you knew God spoke truth to you through the Bible.

Day 2 >>

Hebrews 4:12

"God told me . . ." Have you ever heard people talk as if God were always speaking to them personally? Maybe you've wondered why He doesn't do that for you. To be honest, He doesn't tell me audible things either. But He is talking to you. He is speaking through His Word. This passage tells us that the Bible doesn't just give us facts about God; He actually uses it to help us in our present circumstances. In this chapter, the author quotes some passages from the Old Testament and shows how God uses them to speak to those reading his letter. In the same way, the Holy Spirit will use these ancient texts to speak to you right now. That's why reading the Word of God is so important.

What could God be trying to tell you today from the verse you just read?

Do you ever expect God to speak to you while you are reading Scripture? Why, or why not?

Day 3 >>>
Psalm 19:7-12

Why do we read the Bible and try to live by it? Well, I think most people assume that it's so we can be more righteous. But Verses 7-8 challenge that. Look at all the benefits you get from living according to God's Word: It restores your soul, makes you wise, and brings joy to your heart. Following God doesn't just make you holy; it also makes you happy. David gave us the reason why he got up every day for his quiet time: It made his life work. That's what most people miss about righteousness; it's the best way to live the most joyful life imaginable. That's what God wants for you every day, too. Reading and obeying the Word each morning is a huge part of that.

Think about how living God's way can make your life work better.

Do you have a plan for reading and obeying God's Word daily?

Day 4 >>>>
Matthew 4:1-11

All of us have been tempted before—even Jesus. But look at how He responded in this situation. In each place where Satan tempted Him, Jesus replied with Scripture. Remember, it's living and active. There is power when you fight back, not with your own opinion, but with the unchanging Word of God! A friend of mine at a secular college told me that people always respond differently when you quote Scripture in a discussion. It's one thing to talk as a person; it's another to speak the Word that God wrote. Do you know some verses you could use when tempted or when sharing the gospel with someone? It's more powerful than you know!

Write down five verses you could quote right now.

What are some verses that you need to memorize? As you read the Bible, ask the Lord to show you some Scripture verses that you should memorize.

Day 5 >>>>>
Psalm 119:9-16

Psalm 119 is the longest chapter in the Bible, topping out at 176 verses. (Don't worry; you don't have to read it all now.) The author wrote a stanza for each letter of the Hebrew alphabet. And every bit of it is about the Bible. Throughout it, the author talks about how knowing God's Word helps him to live, to be righteous, to honor God, and to live wisely. That's why he spent so much time thinking about it, meditating on it, and memorizing it. The Word of God was obviously a huge part of his life. Studying led to a passion for the Word. The more you study the Word, the more you'll find this passion as well.

What place does the Bible have in your life?

Do you take it to school?

Do you read it when you're not at church?

Are you studying it?

The more you study God's Word, the more you will be able to experience the joy that the psalmist had in reading the Word.

Preaching and Teaching
Paul's Second Letter to Timothy, Part 2

memory verse

Don't let anyone look down on you because you are young, but set an example for the believers in speech, in life, in love, in faith and in purity. **1 Timothy 4:12**

When you say the word *preaching*, images of a minister with bulging veins spitting hellfire and brimstone may come to mind. If it doesn't, realize that for a lot of people in our culture, that's all they know. Examples of bad preaching are numerous: TV crooks, sandwich board prophets on the side of the road, and finger-pointing bigots. But the preaching and teaching of the Church is much, much different. At the heart of the Church lies the gospel, the message of grace and new life through a relationship with Jesus.

God has chosen to reveal this message to the world through you and me, the followers of Christ. There is no Plan B. We're it! So the preaching and teaching of the Church is a top priority—not just for preachers but for all of us. Knowing this Paul wrote to young disciples like Timothy to make sure they understood the importance of the teaching of the Church. Paul wouldn't be around forever; so he made sure to pass on that message to others who could faithfully preach it to a new generation.

We need to make sure we are receiving good teaching and passing that on to others. Without the teaching of the Church, our beliefs would be reduced to the opinions of the latest charismatic leader. The true message of the Church, though, stands the test of time and is not changed by the ideas of our culture. This week, we'll look at why this is important and how we fit into the task of preaching and teaching today.

Day 1 >

2 Timothy 4:1-5

"Uh, I'm not a minister." As a student, that was my first reaction to this passage. Isn't Paul talking to a preacher? So what does this have to do with me? Realize that though Paul wrote this to Timothy, he meant for it to be read to everyone. And God apparently intended the same thing since He made sure it became a part of the Bible. Even those of us who are not ministers still have a responsibility to tell people about Jesus. Paul reminds us that our culture may one day stop listening, so we have to take every opportunity to preach and teach—no matter where it happens. Keep your eyes open today for a chance to talk about your faith, to correct someone if they speak of Christ falsely, or to encourage someone with Scripture.

If God gave you an opportunity to talk about Christ today, what would you do?

Ask Him for help in speaking about Him today in some way.

Day 2 >>

Acts 14:1-4

Almost everyone today says that if you believe something, then it's true for you. As a result, you can't ever tell anyone they are wrong. But this makes absolutely no sense. How can everyone be right at the same time? The truth is they can't. Someone is right and someone is wrong. Peter stood before the leaders of the Jewish faith claiming the only way to be saved is Jesus—the only way. One of the reasons we have to be serious about hearing good teaching is that a lot of people believe false things. There aren't 8 or 80 or 800 equally correct ways of living. There's only one. So it's important that we make sure we're right. By studying the Bible, listening to good teachers, and challenging bad teaching, we stay on track and avoid silly beliefs . . . like the belief that whatever anyone believes is right.

Is learning the truth important to you, or do you listen only to those people who tell you what you want to hear?

Ask the Lord to help you find the truth and show you any lies you are believing.

Day 3 >>>
Philippians 3:12-16

Have you ever read something in Scripture and said, "I just don't understand"? Me, too. In fact, it happens to everyone at times. Look at this passage. Paul knew that not everyone understood him at first. But he was confident that if his readers would keep working at it, God would help them understand. Sometimes things take time for us to grasp, but don't worry, you're not on your own. Even if you don't feel very good at thinking about biblical things, you can always know the Holy Spirit will help you understand everything you need to know. Our job is to make sure we don't give up after one try. Studying takes time, so don't get discouraged if it's hard at first. It does get easier. Keep at it!

How do you react when you don't get something at first?

Go back to a passage you found hard to comprehend; ask God to help you understand it. Spend time really dwelling on it.

Day 4 >>>>
1 Peter 2:1-3

Growing up is something you really don't have any control over. You go to bed one height and wake up two inches taller. Weird, I know. Spiritually, though, it's not the same. People don't just automatically grow up spiritually. Some people get saved and stay spiritual infants their whole lives. Can you imagine being a baby for 20, 30, or 40 years? Peter was encouraging his church to dig into Scripture because he knew that's the best way for believers to grow in their faith. Without the Word in our lives, we'll never be able to grow up to enjoy all the blessings of walking with God. Don't settle for just being saved; that's just the beginning! Make it a habit to drink in God's

Word. You'll be surprised at how much it helps you.

Is Scripture a chore or a blessing for you to read?

Ask God to give you a hunger for His Word. Keep praying that until it happens.

Day 5 >>>>>
Ephesians 6:10-18

Spiritual warfare is a reality. That doesn't mean that you're going to have to speak weird prayers to cast horned demons out of your locker. It does mean that invisible battles are happening around you daily. How do we get into the fight? Paul talked about arming ourselves with the Lord, and then he spoke of a weapon: the sword of the Spirit. It's the only offensive weapon in the list. The Word of God is our weapon to attack Satan's schemes and protect ourselves. But you have to know it to use it. Reading the Bible, attending Bible studies, and doing what you're doing right now all help you learn how to use Scripture. Learning that skill is crucial to winning the spiritual war we are all in.

Do you make time for Bible study each week?

How can you use what you are learning to help others?

Your Role
Peter and the Priesthood of Believers

memory verse

But you are a chosen people, a royal priesthood, a holy nation, a people belonging to God, that you may declare the praises of him who called you out of darkness into his wonderful light. **1 Peter 2:9**

I don't know how your family did it, but, in order to accommodate all the people at Thanksgiving, we had the kiddie table for anyone under 18. I never liked the kiddie table. I felt I was missing out on everything just because I wasn't old enough. All I wanted was to be a big person! I'm sure the Old Testament Jews felt like that since almost none were allowed in the temple. It wasn't that they weren't old enough; it was that they weren't holy enough. Only the priests could go before God.

This week we're going to be talking about an important belief for Christians called the priesthood of the believer. It means that when you become a Christian you become a priest of sorts. Instead of there being only a few priests to go to God for us, we all get full access to God as believers in Jesus. In the early church, Peter was obviously the one everyone looked to for spiritual guidance. But he was adamant about helping people understand that he wasn't the only one who could commune with God; we all

can through Jesus Christ. Together we are all a "holy priestood."

As a Christian, you have complete access to all the blessings in Christ because He has saved you; you don't need a middleman to go to God on your behalf. But it goes further than that. Because you have this access, God wants to use you like a priest, helping others to find Him. It sounds like a big task, but don't worry. Christ will help you every step of the way.

Day 1 >

1 Peter 2:4-10

When I think about my church, I typically focus on the building. Peter tried to help us understand that we are the building. All of us are living parts of God's temple—designed to be the place God is experienced and worshiped. In the Old Testament, priests lived in that temple, but now every believer is a priest who takes the presence of God with him wherever he goes. So instead of trying to get everyone into a physical temple, God is building a living temple that will literally encompass every Christian . . . everywhere.

How does it change your idea of the Christian life to realize that God wants to use you as a priest?

Ask the Father to help you understand what it means for you to serve Him as one of His priests today.

Day 2 >>

1 John 5:13-15

Oftentimes I've wondered if God hears my prayers. However, the Bible is clear about the answer. In the Old Testament, people went to the temple to give offerings and to worship God. Priests were the mediators between the people and God. Christ changed everything! John was confident

community: The New Testament Church—The Essence of Fellowship

in this passage that God hears our prayers because we are believers. You don't need a priest; you have direct access to God through the Holy Spirit. We now have the privilege that previously only the priests had. That being said, we should be in tune with the Spirit as we pray, asking for things He would approve of, not just things we selfishly want. The Old Testament priests did this and we must do it as well. Rest assured, your prayers are heard.

When you pray, do you seek to be in line with God's will, or do you just ask for whatever you want?

Thank God today for giving us access to Him in a way many others before us never experienced.

Day 3 >>>
James 5:16

Since we're talking about being priests, let's look at this verse again. Does it make more sense to you now? It's important to confess our sins to each other as well as to God, because we are all priests. Each one of us can become the vehicle through which God provides blessings and help. If we never confess to one another, we ignore the fact that God is working through all of us. It also means that, as a priest, I can ask Jesus to pour His love through me to someone else. Sometimes we all wish Jesus was here physically so we could talk to Him, hold onto Him, and lean on Him. James reminded us that this actually happens when we live as priests of the Holy God!

Who are the Christians you can be completely honest with?

Ask Christ to use you to share His love with someone today.

Day 4 >>>>
1 Timothy 2:1-8

Have you ever thought God probably listens to the prayers of really spiritual people, but not to ordinary people? This week, we're learning that ordinary people don't exist. Each of us is important because we are all part of the holy nation of God. Because of this, Paul knew the prayers of the church are incredibly powerful. Never underestimate your place in God's Kingdom. Because you are a child of God, you have the privilege of interceding on behalf of other people. Your prayers actually can bring great change in the lives of your friends and family. Try it and see.

Do you pray as if your prayers will have an impact, or do you pray as if no one really listened? Why?

Spend some time today praying for your friends and family. Pray knowing who you are in Christ.

Day 5 >>>>>
Psalm 84

You may have sung the praise song "Better is One Day" in your church. In case you didn't know, this is where it came from. The psalmist is thinking about being in God's presence and he loves it. In his mind, just being a doorkeeper for God would be better than being anywhere else for thousands of years. The great thing is that, for us, this is a reality! It's not just the chosen few who will get to live in God's presence forever, but anyone who believes in the name of Jesus. God wants you to be in His presence, and because you know Him, you are invited to live with Him forever. Once upon a time, it was only the priests who could get anywhere near God. But now that privilege extends to the entire house of God—including you.

What would it be like to live in God's presence every day?

Do you really believe that God wants you to be that close to Him?

Believe it because He does!

The Church Prepared: John's Vision

memory verse

Therefore, since we are surrounded by such a great cloud of witnesses, let us throw off everything that hinders and the sin that so easily entangles, and let us run with perseverance the race marked out for us.

Hebrews 12:1

Have you ever seen a dead church? It's kind of depressing. I pass one regularly going across town. It's small, and the cemetery next to it is the only part that still gets visited. Through an open doorway, you can see the pews and where the pulpit used to be. Those windows might have once held stained glass, but the church is dead. No one meets there anymore, and who knows what happened to the people. It's a sad commentary that this happened. It ought to remind us of the spiritual battle we are all in. And it should make us perk up and stay alert to Satan's plans to destroy us if he can.

But Jesus will never abandon a church without a fight. Revelation is the story of a vision John had while exiled on the island of Patmos. Through this vision, a message was sent to seven churches, challenging and encouraging them to stand firm. The stakes were huge; they could have lost it all or gained a crown of glory.

Jesus is returning, and He will do everything He can to make sure we are prepared before He comes. That means He sometimes has to tell us things that are hard to hear. But it's for our own good, and when we obey His commands, we can be confident that He will bring about all that He has promised. This week, we're going to examine what Jesus said to those seven churches . . . and find out how we can protect our own.

Day 1 >
Revelation 2:1-7

It's possible to get so caught up in what you are doing that you forget why you are doing it. This can even happen to us as believers. Even when we are doing a lot of spiritual things, if we forget why we are doing them, it does us no good. Jesus was telling the church in Ephesus that keeping everyone pure is important; however, the main thing is to be in love with Jesus. It's easier to drift away from this than we think. We can do godly things but forget about God. How about you? Is your main focus being in a love relationship with Jesus? It's not enough to look spiritual; we have to *be* spiritual.

What is your first love?

If this message was for you, what would you need to repent of to make Jesus your first love?

Day 2 >>
Revelation 2:8-11

If Jesus knows it's going to happen, then why doesn't He stop it? Because all is not as it seems. They may seem poor in the world's eyes, but Jesus is revealing to them that they have treasures unlike anything this world has seen. Even when they undergo persecution, God is using their suffering for His glory and to draw people to Himself. When we face harsh circumstances, we always have to remember that there is more going on than meets the eye. To us, it may seem bad, but our future glory will far outweigh the suffering we endure here. This requires faith, for sure, but the fact that God sent them this message shows that He is in control and has a plan and a future for them. We can never let our circumstances determine whether we'll be faithful or not. We must decide to be faithful no matter what.

What was comforting about this letter for those in Smyrna?

What will you have to endure today to follow Christ?

Pray for yourself and for all those who will face persecution today.

Day 3 >>>
Revelation 2:12-17

Can you imagine hearing this from God Himself: "Satan lives in your neighborhood"? The church in Pergamum must have had strong faith to live in that kind of environment. But even they had compromised. They had resisted Satan in some areas but had allowed some other sins to creep in. This is a common problem. When you are already standing firm on the really big issues, it is some-

times easy to fudge on the seemingly smaller matters. Why worry about your language when you have to stand firm against premarital sex and drug use? But just because we are faithful in big areas, that doesn't give us freedom to compromise. Jesus is sternly reminding them to keep alert in all areas.

Are there parts of your life you have allowed to be less than what God desires?

Ask God to reveal to you any place in your life that you have compromised with sin.

Day 4 >>>>
Revelation 2:18-29

You may not understand all the details of what was going on in Thyatira, but you can get the gist of it. The majority of the church was growing but someone encouraged them to go astray into odd sexual practices and secret rituals. Everyone loves secrets, so this had apparently snagged a lot of the Thyatirans. Jesus reminded us that even Christians will be called to account for our actions. If we love Christ, we must stay alert and avoid sin in any form.

Is there anyone in your church or school who is tempting people to do things that would dishonor Christ—even a little bit?

How would you confront someone who was doing this in your church?

How would you protect yourself and others from their influence?

Pray for wisdom in facing such situations now—or in the future—if you are called on do so.

Day 5 >>>>>>
Revelation 3:1-6

This would have been a depressing message to hear from God. Or maybe it was just the kind of wake-up call this church needed. It makes no difference what people see on the outside. Even if people think we have a great church and come faithfully every week, that doesn't mean we are truly alive. The goal of a church—or even your youth group—is not to be popular but to be rooted in Christ. How can you tell which is which? Well, when you talk about your church, do you talk about how God is changing people and what He is calling you to do as a church? Or do you talk about who came, what they did, and how much fun it was—without referring to Christ at all? It could be a life-and-death question.

If Jesus never showed up at your next church meeting, would anyone notice He was gone.

community: The New Testament Church—The Essence of Fellowship

The Church Eternal
The New Jerusalem

The Lord is not slow in keeping his promise, as some understand slowness. He is patient with you, not wanting anyone to perish, but everyone to come to repentance.

2 Peter 3:9

Harps, clouds, and white—lots of white. That's the picture most of us have when we think about heaven. To be honest, heaven has always seemed kind of gaudy to me. I mean. . . pearly gates, streets of gold? If this is our picture of heaven, then it's not going to be much of a motivational factor in the life of the church. Who wants to go to a place where you have to sit in a choir loft for 4 billion years?

The truth is that heaven is going to be a place more magnificent than your wildest dreams. The Bible says that when Christ returns and takes us home, He is going to make everything new. All of the pain and frustration we deal with now—and all the things that cause them—will be gone. Can you imagine what it will be like to not have to deal with sin anymore, to never have to wrestle with your thoughts again, to live in a place where you can see Jesus with your very own eyes?

If heaven seems boring to you, then you don't have a very clear picture of it. This week, we're going to look at the eternal future of the church. We're going to have to use our imaginations, but the Holy Spirit has given us some guidelines in Scripture to help us understand a place that is so amazing that we don't even have the words to describe it.

Day 1 >

Revelation 21:1-8

If we see a problem with something, it's almost natural to want to fix it and make it better. Now, imagine that happening on a global scale. When Jesus returns, everything is going to be changed; He is going to make everything new. How do you improve on a sunset? Or a galaxy? The big improvement will be that God will eradicate sin once and for all, and we will be able to live with Him as we were intended to. But God is not going to simply patch up the old world; He is going to fix it once and for all. Let's do an exercise today. God gave you an imagination for a reason. Use it to try to picture what that might be like, and then remember that nothing we can dream up will even come close to what God has in store for us. Buckle up; it's coming soon!

Day 2 >>

1 Corinthians 15:35-49

We don't talk about this enough. Most of us know that our souls will go to be with the Lord when we die, but we often forget that Jesus promised us a bodily resurrection. Jesus Himself was raised body and soul from the dead, and so we will be— body and soul. How will that work? Well, no one knows for sure, but Paul reminds us here that it will happen.

community: The New Testament Church—The Essence of Fellowship

You are going to have some sort of physical body that is completely spiritual; one that will never wear out, get old, or die. It will even be glorious! We will walk into heaven, not float. And while you won't get wings (we will not become angels), you won't be disappointed with your new appearance!

If our bodies will be raised, as well as our souls, should we take care of our bodies more than we do?

Spend some time thinking about what a new spiritual body might be like.

Day 3 >>>
Revelation 2:17; 21:2-3

Sometimes it may seem as if God were a million miles away from us. Those are the times when we really have to live by faith—knowing that His presence is with us even when we can't feel it. But when we go to live with Him, it's going to be very different. Look at the images in these verses. God will give you a special name that will be known only to you and the Lord. It's a special name you will share together. Then we are described as a bride meeting her husband at the altar. It's a very intimate image. God won't be like a king leading his people from afar. He will be among us. We'll get to see Him, and we'll have a relationship that is closer than anything we've ever known.

Try to imagine what it will be like to experience God in this way.

Since God wants to be as close to you as possible, even now, how can you grow closer to Him today?

Day 4 >>>>
Revelation 20:11-15; 21:8

Charles Spurgeon said that if you ever preach about hell, it should be done with tears in your eyes. The bliss of heaven is rivaled only by the nightmarish reality of hell: eternal separation from God. There is no middle ground. Those who choose to reject an eternity with God are doomed to a life forever without Him. Does God purposefully send people here? The great Christian writer C. S. Lewis once said something that appears to be a good answer to this question. He stated that all those who are in hell choose it. In other words, they either choose to be with God or choose to be without Him, and God will honor their choice—even if it is hell. But if this is the option for those who don't know Christ, we should be doing everything in our powers to make sure they make the right choice.

Who do you know who is not saved? Ask God for an opportunity to talk to that person about a relationship with Christ.

community: The New Testament Church—The Essence of Fellowship

Day 5 >>>>>
Revelation 22:1-6

A lot of Revelation is symbolic, so we don't know exactly what heaven will look like. However, these passages help us understand what it will be like generally. Notice, here, where we are. There's the tree of life from Genesis, but now it's not in a garden; it's in the middle of a city. What started with Adam and Eve has turned into the church made up of believers from all nations. When we get there, we will live in a community where there is no fear, no violence, no pain, no mistrust, and no oppression. No one will ever mistreat anyone else; you will never be laughed at, ignored, left out, abused, or mistreated ever again. Imagine living with a group of people like that—where everyone you meet is as close and trustworthy as your best friend. Now that's a place worth waiting for! Does your youth group or church look more like this new community than the rest of the world? Why, or why not?

How can you help form that kind of community on Earth now?

A Final Word

The journal read like a Hollywood action movie, didn't it? What a story! Think back on all you've read: the Holy Spirit coming at Pentecost; persecution, imprisonment, and beatings experienced by the Apostles; the death-on-the-spot of Ananias and Saphira; Stephen's murder; Paul's conversion, missionary journeys, shipwreck, and ultimate imprisonment in Rome, and so much more. Trying to comprehend all this information is like drinking from a fire hose—it's almost too much to handle. But more than just a collection of great stories, there were some solid principles to be learned from each lesson.

The story of the New Testament Church teaches us so much about being a member of Christ's Church. We are not designed to stand alone. As followers of Christ we are meant to live within the body of believers, contributing our gifts and prayers to the church, and working to spread the good news of Christ throughout the world. We are meant to put all our energies into uplifting our fellow believers as well as those who have never heard the gospel. But be reminded, you are not just a member of your local church but of the global Church, the family of Christians everywhere. These are the lessons of the New Testament Church.

Hopefully you have learned these lessons this year. God calls His children to a higher standard. By focusing on what Christian community is, as you have done the last 48 weeks, you have learned what it means to live the Christian life in the context of the church and of the world. And through the power of the Holy Spirit, you have the opportunity to live the same kind of exciting, fruitful life seen in the Book of Acts. Allow God to take control of your life . . . and hold on for the ride! There is no telling what you'll experience.